Praise for *Mindfulnes*

"Read this—now. Baran ... the world's greatest thinkers."

    —*O, The Oprah Magazine*

"This book is a treasury of wisdom that brings us to a deeper understanding of how being present—of living in the present moment—allows us to experience life more fully and brings us contentment in our everyday lives."

    —Rodney Yee, author of *Yoga: The Poetry of the Body* and *Moving Toward Balance: 8 Weeks of Yoga with Rodney Yee*

"This book is for everyone who wants to be free and happy here and now, This is a profound and exciting collection of wisdom that you can read every day."

    —Jack Canfield, coauthor of *Chicken Soup for the Soul*

"Whether you are on a spiritual path or are simply looking for inspiration, this wonderful treasury offers 365 days of wisdom that will last a lifetime."

    —Lama Surya Das

"If you love *The Power of Now,* this book is for you. This is the first time that such wisdom has been drawn together from so many thrillingly diverse sources. Boith fun to read and transformational."

    —Raphael Cushnir, author of *Setting Your Heart on Fire*

"This diversity at its best, shining facets of wisdom, each brilliant with its own intensity."

    —Helen Palmer, author of *The Ennegram*

"The right words at the right time can pierce our protections like an arrow. This book is full of deadly, life-giving arrows. Open it at any page and be ready to die to who you thought you were."

—Roger Housden, author of *Ten Poems to Change Your Life*

"*The* best compliation of short wisdom teachings in print—the one spiritual book to keep on your nightstand. To put together a contemporary collection such as this requires an editor like Josh Baran who recognizes from his own direct experience the most timeless spiritual truths."

—Catherine Ingram, author of *Passionate Presence* and *In the Footsteps of Gandhi*

"This exquisite handbook for enlightenment contains more distilled power, wisdom, and truth than anything I've read in years. No religion, no guru, no boundaries, no practice—merely the essential teachings of liberation here and now, radical in its global scope, transcendent in simplicity. This book will change lives."

—Mark Matousek, author of *Sex Death Enlightenment* and *The Boy He Left Behind*

"*A* wise and discriminating collection that points infallibily to what is true. I never want to be without these teachings."

—Kate Wheeler, author of *When Mountains Walked* and *Nixon under the Bodhi Tree*

"In this stunning collection, Baran has gathered 365 ways to live in the present moment with peace and awareness."

—*Spirituality and Health*

mindfulness

day by day

how to find peace in the present moment

JOSH BARAN

Foreword by Sharon Salzberg and Susan Piver

HAMPTON ROADS

dedicated to
a new generation of
mindful explorers

Copyright © 2018 by Josh Baran
Foreword copyright © 2018 by Sharon Salzberg and Susan Piver

All rights reserved. No part of this publication may be reproduced or transmitted in any form or by any means, electronic or mechanical, including
photocopying, recording, or by any information storage and retrieval system, without permission in writing from Red Wheel/Weiser, LLC. Reviewers
may quote brief passages. Previously published in 2008, 2012 as *Tao of
Now* by Hampton Roads Publishing, ISBN 978-1-57174-686-3.

Cover design by Kathryn Sky-Peck
Typeset in ITC Fenice

Hampton Roads Publishing Company, Inc.
Charlottesville, VA 22906
Distributed by Red Wheel/Weiser, LLC
www.redwheelweiser.com

Sign up for our newsletter and special offers by going to
www.redwheelweiser.com/newsletter.

ISBN: 978-1-57174-841-6
Library of Congress Control Number: 2018930613

Printed in Canada
MAR

10   9   8   7   6   5   4   3   2   1

Contents

With the "I" elminated . . .
this is *Nirvana*—here and now

THE BUDDHA

It is right in your face.
This moment,
the whole thing is handed to you.

YUANWU

You search for God in heaven and earth, but
you don't know the one who is right before your
eyes, because you don't know how to search
into *this very moment*.

JESUS

Foreword

In this collection, Josh Baran presents mindfulness in a very direct and useful way. It contains simple daily pointers—not abstract, not lengthy. You don't have to tangle with these insights. There are selections here both spiritual and secular, but they all point to the same truth that is beyond any one approach or belief system. You can open this collection to any page and find something that will connect with what you are facing right now, or what might show up in the coming days or weeks. There's very little jargon. It doesn't feel overly religious. This book serves a real and valuable service.

As authors, we both can appreciate the art of curating quotations and short offerings. These insights are not just filler, but serve an important purpose. Josh's book is full of these impactful insights.

The essential message of *Mindfulness Day by Day* is inspiration. So many of these pieces directly inspire readers to stop and look for meaning in our everyday life.

It's a lot of responsibility to curate somebody's adventure. Josh cares so much and has done a wonderful job of gathering these pieces. I have heard stories over the years of people who stumbled across this book at just the right moment, and just one phrase, one piece, one little paragraph gave them a spark of encouragement—the right inspiration at the right time.

Making a big change in our lives usually involves times of really blowing it, then picking it up again. That sense of common humanity is always moving—here we are, all in this together. These wise insights remind us of our frailty and our vulnerability as well as our capacity to continue to grow and change and see things in different ways. These pointers are immediately useful, showing us how we can bring more attention and compassion into our lives, into our relationships, right now. It's not a surprise that this book has been around for fifteen years. It doesn't age, and now it speaks to a whole new generation of meditators.

Although Josh's book is rooted in mindfulness and awareness, it also addresses the qualities of kindness and compassion. Many of the pieces in the book show us what compassion looks like in a wide variety of situations. The stories in the book make mindfulness and compassion come alive.

Echoing throughout this work are spiritual teachers, some living, some dead, as well as artists, poets, musicians, regular folks: people of all stripes who appreciate what it means to pay attention to the present moment and are working on the same issues and obstacles as we are. This chorus of voices gives us a sense of the bigger tribe—of all people. We are all trying to wake up and find meaning. This process is timeless and borderless.

These pieces help to connect us to something bigger than our immediate dilemma. They provide us with perspective as well as confidence in our own capacity to deal with things. We are not so alone. Josh points to our being part of a larger family of beings. Instead of feeling isolated, we can feel connected in a bigger way. These connections can be supported by art and music and poetry and wise words, a chorus of interconnections.

Whether our situation is positive or challenging, we often forget to take a moment to appreciate both. We skate right by them. The value of the short insights in Josh's book is that they invite us to stop for a moment. They tell us to take a minute and look now. *Look now.*

—*Sharon Salzberg and Susan Piver*

Introduction

Stop. Now.

Whether you know it or not, you are at the end of your search for relief, peace, and meaning in your life. No more seeking. No more wandering. No more waiting. The peace you seek is hiding in plain sight. An open secret.

This treasury of insights, a chorus of the present moment sung by ancient and modern voices that span time, distance, religion, tradition, and culture—is an invitation to become aware of where you are, who you are, as you are—right here, right now. The wisdom contained in this book points the way to life freed from the burdensome stories of your past and the worries and expectations of an imagined future.

Stop now and look. It is in front of your nose. In the palm of your hand. In the light in your eyes. In the taste on your tongue. You may have ignored this truth your entire life, but you have never been apart from it even for a single moment. Nothing is required. No new meditation practices, therapies, ceremonies, or gurus. No path. Everything you need is already here, unfolding in every instant. Right here, right now.

How This Book Came to Be

I begin with a memory. I am 14 years old. Along with several close friends, I am attending a concert by the folk music group Peter, Paul and Mary near the beach in Santa Monica, California. I have been looking forward to this event for months. We have good seats and I love the songs, but for some reason, in the middle of the concert, I become acutely preoccupied with the thoughts in my mind.

What had been background chatter suddenly leaps into the foreground of my attention. My thoughts are constant, loud and random, telling stories about the concert, rehearsing what I will say to friends later, comparing this event to previous concerts, and on and on. I feel as if I am trapped on a carnival ride, spinning out of control. I also notice a sense of separation from the world, as if imprisoned inside a glass box. This is a seminal moment in my life: from this point on, I will become intensely and increasingly aware of this non-stop mental turmoil. And it is a desire for relief from this inner chaos that initiates my quest.

I began my search alone, digging into philosophy, religion, and psychology books. At one point, I found myself drawn to

Asian mysticism. When I discovered the Buddha's description of *samsara*, the human state of confusion and suffering, I felt that he was directly addressing me. What a relief to learn that I was not alone after all! And what a thrill to discover that there was a way to wake up, to realize *nirvana*—a state of peace accessible to anyone.

A deep yearning for the truth took over my life. I began to devour tales of Zen monks, Tibetan yogis, and Indian sages. I longed for first-hand realization. I was one throbbing question mark: Who or what am *I?* What is *this?*—*this* reality, *this* feeling of "me," *this* life and death, *this* moment? There seemed something enormously significant hidden, urging me to find it.

By age 19, I was a full-time seeker. It was the late 1960s. A spiritual renaissance was unfolding in the West. Ancient wisdom filled the air, antithetical to the current American culture: the Vietnam War, materialism, and Richard Nixon. Swamis, Sufi masters, whirling dervishes, and Buddhist sages found audiences in North America and Europe. I attended every spiritual workshop I could find and scoured bookstore shelves, hunting for the latest works on mysticism. After months of bouncing between traditions and teachers, I decided that the only way to get to the heart of the matter was to choose one path and devote myself to it. My choice was Zen Buddhism.

Zen seemed the quickest and most direct way to understanding, even though I had heard that Zen monasteries were legendary boot camps where masters would push their students to the breaking point. I joined a newly established community in California, composed entirely of fellow Westerners. I shaved my head, donned black monastic robes, and entered into this unknown world of meditation and discipline. For the next eight years, I would live as a Zen monk and priest.

There is an old Zen saying: "With the ideal comes the actual." My Zen experience was complex—enlightening in many ways and "en-darkening" in others. The demanding routine and meditation practice enabled me to become more focused and mindful in my daily activities. I began to notice the way my mind created confusion and clinging. Soon I had glimpses of the peace that I had read about.

But as the years passed, my eyes opened to the shadow side of the Zen community. As my fellow monks and I drove ourselves in the name of devotion, we began to repress personal feelings. Questioning was not merely discouraged but strictly forbidden. Total obedience to the teacher eclipsed every other consideration. I found myself ignoring my feelings and denying my doubts.

At first, I blamed myself for these "negative" feelings, attributing them to my own shortcomings. If only I meditated harder and surrendered more fully, then everything would be perfect. But I soon came to realize that the problem lay not in me but with the harsh and unkind culture of the monastery. It took me the better part of a year, but I finally mustered the courage to walk out the door. I later learned that my experience was not at all unusual; by the early 1980s, hundreds of spiritual groups started to unravel under the weight of their authoritarian cultures.

Yet, even after my departure, the internal questioning that had brought me to Zen in the first place was still inside me, burning more urgently than ever. For the next 15 years, I steered clear of spiritual organizations, continuing my exploration on my own. Sometimes enlightenment seemed further away, others times a bit closer—yet always out of reach. No matter how many hours I meditated, distracting thoughts persisted.

At times, I had powerful experiences, including intense states of bliss. I would then try to hold on to them, only to see them change or fade away. Was I really advancing on the path? Was I getting any closer? After two decades of meditating and searching, I still felt like that 14-year-old at the Peter, Paul and Mary concert. After so much time meditating on my own, I still felt confused and wanted some help.

During this period of my life, friends had periodically urged me to journey to Nepal to receive Dzogchen teachings from a revered master, Tulku Urgyen. Dzogchen, a tradition of Tibetan Buddhism, emphasizes direct personal experience. For centuries, these teachings were zealously kept secret and only given to accomplished students who had completed decades of meditation practice. Fortunately, Tulku Urgyen's approach was different. He not only believed in sharing knowledge with Westerners, he did so at the beginning of instruction.

One day, I found myself jetting halfway around the world to Nepal. I made my way to Tulku Urgyen's temple, perched high above the Kathmandu Valley, where I joined a small group of other Western students. Each morning we sat with Tulku Urgyen in his small room, where he imparted traditional Dzogchen teachings, "pointing out" the true nature of the mind.

So powerfully and directly did Tulku Urgyen communicate this timeless and immediate reality, that I found my "self" instantly stopped cold. There were no fireworks, no thunder—just the sudden, obvious, stunning realization of the pure awareness that I had overlooked my entire life, not hidden or elsewhere.

In the face of this presence or *nowness*, all seeking, wandering, and waiting vanished before my eyes. I saw how much of my life's energies had been focused on looking forward to some imagined future, rather than simply celebrating the all-pervasive present: trying to get "there" instead of being "here." My previous years of forced meditation and effort seemed, in retrospect, useless. All I needed was to take to heart Tulku Urgyen's words, "Simply let be in naturalness without technique, without artifice."

Mystics have shared this same insight for thousands of years. In the words of Zen Master Hakuin:

> At this moment, is there anything lacking?
> Nirvana is right here now before our eyes.
> *This* place is the lotus land.
> *This* body now is the Buddha.

The second line is also translated, "Nirvana is immediate"—not hidden, distant, or in the future, but right now, before your face—*this* body, *this* place.

When I returned to America, I found that I could no longer stomach many of the spiritual books in my apartment. They seemed filled with unquestioned assumptions that glorified seeking, wishful thinking, and magical experiences. Many authors gave lip service to the concept of living in the present moment, but then proceeded to promote more fruitless seeking. Before Nepal,

I had bought into the New Age cliché that all paths lead to the top of the mountain. Now, I saw that these "paths" often served to create more layers of illusion. I hungered for words that were alive with realization and that reflected the timeless view that Tulku Urgyen had pointed out. Slowly, I began to gather quotations and writings that hit the nail on the head.

My collection began with teachings from the Zen and Tibetan Buddhist traditions, and soon expanded to include wisdom from Indian masters, Christian mystics, Sufi poets, Jewish rabbis, and Western sages. Each selection embodied an outlook often referred to as "nonduality," which is not exclusive to any single religious tradition and which transcends any doctrine or system.

Nonduality reflects the understanding of the unity of all things. Self/other, nirvana/samsara, form/emptiness, body/mind, past/future —all are actually the same essence, having one taste. When the Buddha says, "This is the All"; when Meister Eckhart writes, "Everything tastes like God"; and when Ramana Maharshi teaches, "There is only the Self"—these words all express the same realization.

As I gathered these teachings, I began to include pieces from poets, songwriters, artists, screenwriters, and scientists. I came across inspired accounts from ordinary people who experienced this truth in their everyday lives. Many were not particularly spiritual or religious, many were seekers, but suddenly, for no apparent reason, they saw clearly and directly for an instant.

After years of gathering these nuggets, I strung them together and now joyfully offer them to you.

The insights that follow span thousands of years and yet all express the same timeless present. While each selection stands alone, together they create a remarkable and colorful chorus. This book contains many pieces and insights from traditional religious or spiritual sources, as well as many from very unusual characters—who may not have been "religious" at all. I have been particularly fascinated by mavericks who occasionally and unexpectedly arise outside of any tradition or box including Tony Parson, Steven Harrison, Scott Morrison or Byron Katie. Recently, Dr. Jill Bolte Taylor captivated the audience at the TED conference in California by relating a riveting account of her profound awakening that took place during a severe stroke. As her body began to fail, she simultaneously experienced a spontaneous sense of awareness/nowness/peace.

Opinions vary widely as to who is realized, authentic, or "mystically correct." Please do not regard this book as a Who's Who of Enlightenment. I have included these passages solely because they strike home for me. Some stop me dead in my tracks; others bring tears or goose bumps. The material is organized in a manner that encourages spontaneous exploration. Jump in anywhere and just read a page or two. The selections come from a wide variety of sources, ranging from the highly traditional to the wildly iconoclastic.

As such, it is only natural to expect differences and contradictions, and these reflect the immense paradox of addressing the reality that is entirely beyond words, concepts, thoughts, and time. This is particularly apparent with regard to such issues as effort, meditation, and spiritual practices. For example, the debate over effort—*doing* versus *not doing* as a means to realization—has been going on for thousands of years. On the one hand, many traditional sages teach that the natural and effortless state of awareness can only be realized *after* decades of effort. This approach requires serious training, meditation, and practice. At the other end of the spectrum, sages such as Krishnamurti and Poonjaji regard *any* intentional effort to wake up or quiet the mind as counterproductive—an expression of the "I" locked in the illusions of goals, progress, and achievement.

It is my observation that many people are beginning to see spirituality in a more integrated way—focusing on relaxed effort in the present moment, without trying to achieve anything or make something happen. It is an open, welcoming, and honest inquiry into thoughts, feelings, and experiences, without avoidance or any attempt to fix or alter them. This gentle awareness encompasses every moment of life and illuminates what is true and what is false. The only spiritual "practice" required is to merely recognize this natural state—now, and now, and now.

As you go through these passages, you will notice many diverse views. As you read the selection, try setting aside any beliefs you may hold. Let each insight speak for itself. Notice every time your mind says, "Yes, BUT . . ." Are you thinking that realization is only for saints and very special people but not for you? Do you feel that you cannot possibly understand right now, but only at some point in the distant future or many lifetimes from now? I call these "not me, not now" thoughts. When such notions arise in your mind chatter, question them. Try asking yourself, "Who would I be without these thoughts?" Notice what happens when you believe these thoughts.

The pages ahead contain many examples of *self-inquiry*, a special kind of questioning that differs radically from the normal question and answer process. Typically, when asked a question, your answer is based on past experience, what you already know or believe. In contrast, *self-inquiry* is an expression of "beginner's mind," which has no past and is fresh and open in this moment. The Zen tradition is legendary for this, particularly in the use of questions, dialogues, and paradoxical stories called *koans*, such as, "What is the sound of one hand?" Ramana Maharshi suggested asking yourself the question, "Who am I?" And Byron Katie has created an in-depth inquiry process that begins with the question, "Is it true?"

The insights contained in these pages may help dispel beliefs that keep you from realizing that what you seek is already here.

You *are* the Buddha—Now!
Not later.

Not *after* anything.
Not *after* some special experience.
Peace is completely now.
Contentment is now.
Joy is now.
The end of your suffering is now.
What are you waiting for?
You can see this immediately or postpone it for
30 years.
Why wait for some future now?
Stop, look and listen now.
The Tao is now.

To spiritual practitioners who have been "on the path" for a long time, I hope that this book can serve as a reminder that they may be sleepwalking. I know about sleepwalking from first-hand experience. I have seen how any spiritual discipline can become a numbing routine, postponing the joy and freshness that is always available right-here-now. A seasoned meditator recently said to me, "On my deathbed, I hope to have some experience of enlightenment." Decades of meditation had not made awakening any more real for her; it was still an imaginary future dream.

Since the truth of right-here-now is available to everyone everywhere, you might ask if there is any value in traveling to Asia, becoming a meditation student, or finding a master. Teachers and mentors often play a transformative role in our lives. They certainly have in my life. In wise hands, spiritual practices can be beneficial. Belonging to a spiritual group or network can provide a sense of support and community. On the other hand, any teaching or practice, no matter how profound or ancient, can remain merely conceptual or descend into dogmatic religion or blind devotion. Communities can become cults. As for enlightened masters, there is no shortage of holy hucksters.

While it is not my role to direct you, a word to the wise (and you are wise whether you consciously realize it or not): You are the sole supreme authority over your life. This is the only life you know right now. Waking up is about your individual and personal undoing of the long-held assumptions that prevent you from seeing what you really are. Whether you are sitting in a cave in Tibet or standing at a bus stop in Hoboken, you can actualize this clear seeing at any moment, right-here-now. Recognize what is right in front of you. Wherever you go or whatever you do, bear in mind that home is where you always are, where you start and where you end. Peace is found *on this breath.*

Words can never describe the true nature of how things are. They can only point. As you read these insights, try not getting trapped in the phrases and concepts, no matter how mind-blowing or poetic they may seem. Instead, stop and look. See where these words point and then drop them—completely. This is all about seeing and has nothing to do with beliefs. What the Buddha, mystics, or Zen Masters realized has nothing to do with your own understanding. In the end, what others say is all just story and hearsay. As Rumi wrote, "Don't listen to what I say, as though these words came from an inside and went to an outside. My words are fire."

May the words in this book whisper to you with the intimacy

of a lover. When Joshu asks, "Who are you?" ask yourself this question as if for the first time. When Patrul asks, "Do you hear the dogs barking?" listen carefully. And when Woody Guthrie sings, "This great eternal moment is my great eternal dawn," watch the sun rise with your own eyes.

JOSH BARAN, NEW YORK CITY, SUMMER 2008

In
This
Moment

Before you dive into this book, I invite you to stop for a moment and guide your attention to your experience right now. Do this as if you are a newborn child, noticing everything for the very first time. Bring your attention to your breath as it moves in and out of your chest and nostrils. Hear the sounds around you, whatever they may be: cars honking, dogs barking, the wind in the trees.

Notice your eyes as they move back and forth across this page. Feel the weight of this book in your hands, the sensation of your back against the chair, your feet on the ground, and your clothes against your skin. As you read these words, you may be silently saying them to yourself. At the same time, thoughts may appear—streams of words, images, bits of conversation. Be aware of these as they come and go, appear and disappear, one leading to the next.

All of this is being experienced specifically by someone— you. Who is this "you?"

Take a moment to explore this. *Who* is reading these words right now? *Who* is seeing and hearing? These questions might seem odd or absurd and the answer obvious: "Me . . . *I am reading these words*, of course. I am sitting in this chair." So, who is this "I" that is reading and hearing right now? You might answer with your name, age, race, physical description, and so on. You might define your "I" by speaking about your past, where you were born, or your resume or credentials. But exactly who or what is this "I" that occupies the center of every instant in your life? In what ways is this "I" special and unique, distinct from all the other "I"s in the world? What do you *really* know about this "I"?

You may be so immersed in the automatic, habitual, and non-stop stream of "I" thoughts, that you are mostly unaware of them. You may have never even considered what this ongoing drama really is.

Notice that this "I" is a non-stop storyteller, spinning tales of the past, the present, and the future—constantly editing, interpreting, and directing this inner movie.

Take a few quiet minutes. Begin to notice how the "I" shows up ("I am . . . I feel . . . I want . . . I need . . . I should . . ."). Observe each thought as it arises. Now, ask yourself, "Who is thinking these thoughts?" Is there a "somebody" thinking them? Do not look to past experiences, assumptions, or anything you have ever read or heard. Rely only on your direct experience in this moment. Who is thinking these thoughts? Who is reading these words right now?

Now notice the awareness itself that is inquiring into this "I." What is this? Where is it located? Where does it come from? Look closely. This awareness/knowing is not the "I" itself. The awareness is not thoughts. It is not a state, a place, an object, or a concept.

This knowing is clear and transparent. It contains and permeates everything. This sense of being is always present, unchanging, and does not come or go.

This presence-aliveness is intimately here and wholly now without past or future, beyond all concepts and opposites. No need to close your eyes, meditate, go into some altered or higher consciousness, or even "try" to see this. Just remain relaxed and attentive. Simply observe this "*is*-ness." It has many names: the Tao, Nirvana, No-Self, Buddha Nature, the Now, Original Mind, Enlightenment, the Unborn.

The Tao of Now celebrates this natural awakened state—wide open and available in every moment. This book celebrates what you are now.

About the Commentary

At the end of some of the selections in the book, I have written some brief personal comments or reflections. These remarks are intended to direct your attention back to the present moment. Poetic inspiration is fine, but my hope is that this book will be a daily useful tool that directly points out what is true right now. I encourage you to engage in your own dialogue with these living insights.

About
the
Bibliography

A complete source list of the passages in this collection may be found in the bibliography (Sources and Permissions) at the back of the book, which also includes relevant websites, so you can explore specific writings and teachings.

Note

This book was originally published in 2003 under the title *365 Nirvana Here and Now*. This new edition has been renamed *The Tao of Now* and is slightly revised with some additional selections.

The Tao of Now

Daily
Wisdom

All you who seek the Way
Please,
Do not waste this moment now.

ZEN TEACHING

This is the time. This is the place. This is the vastness. Right here is paradise. Always. Always.

BYRON KATIE

At this moment, is there anything lacking?
Nirvana is right here now before our eyes.
This place is the lotus land.
This body now is the Buddha.

HAKUIN

Hold up your hands before your eyes.
You are looking at the hands of God.

RABBI LAWRENCE KUSHNER

What we are looking for
is what is looking.

ST. FRANCIS OF ASSISI

3

The Lost Necklace

No special effort is necessary to realize the Self. All efforts are for eliminating the present obscuration of the Truth.

A lady is wearing a necklace around her neck. She forgets it, imagines it to be lost and impulsively looks for it here, there and everywhere. Not finding it, she asks her friends if they have found it anywhere, until one kind friend points to her neck and tells her to feel the necklace around her neck. The seeker does so and feels happy that the necklace is found.

Again, when she meets other friends, they ask her if her lost necklace was found. She says, "yes" to them, as if it were lost and later recovered. Her happiness at re-discovering it round her neck is the same as if some lost property was recovered. In fact, she never lost it nor recovered it. And yet she was once miserable and now she is happy. So also with the Realization of the Self.

RAMANA MAHARSHI

Awakening is not a faraway secret. The peace you seek is right-here-now. A guru or a Buddha cannot give it to you. Just see clearly in this moment. As you read these pages, keep this in mind.

A monk asked, "What is Buddha?"
The master said, "Who are you?"

JOSHU

In the present moment, we have no interest in past sages or future promises. If you want to know what the Buddha is, look to your own mind. Who are you now?

Original Face Contemplation

Sitting quietly, feel what sits there.

Explore this body you sit in.

Observe the scintillating field of sensation we call the body.

Notice sensation's wordless quality.

Its sense of simply being humming throughout the body.

Go within sensation to that subtle presence by which the sensation is known. Feel the sensation within sensation.

Settle into that sense of being, of aliveness vibrating in each cell.

Rest in being.

Just sit quietly and know. Let awareness sink into itself. Know what knows.

Experience directly that sense by which you imagine you exist.

Enter it wholeheartedly. Sit in the center of that hum.

Does it have a beginning? Does it have an ending?

Or is there just a sense of endless being, unborn and undying?

Don't ask the mind, which always limits itself with definitions, ask the heart, which cannot name it but always is it.

Rest in being.

STEPHEN LEVINE

Let sitting meditation be simple. Don't try to be spiritual or accomplished. Just sit without a goal or any special strategy. Thoughts come and go like clouds in the silent sky.

And I Was Time

There is a classic Zen koan that asks you to describe your own original face, the one you had before you were born. I've never come as close to being able to answer that question as I did the year my mother died. She had cancer and became bedridden for a very short time. During the last three or four days of her life, she began to change outwardly a great deal. She lost weight rapidly, and her skin began to tighten and become less wrinkled. She, in fact, began to appear transformed into someone very relaxed and quite young. She began to closely resemble the old photos of her that I had seen, pictures taken when she was in her early twenties. She was like a young woman who had dyed her hair gray, as if on a whim—a restless echo of happier times.

When I looked at her, I felt swallowed up in some kind of enormous gift. It was as if I had been given the opportunity of seeing my mother as she was before I was born. Time seemed to stand still. And time became exceptionally real for me, only because it ceased to exist. The woman before me was time. And I was time. And the room was time.

GARY THORP

You
Are
the
Truth

You are the truth from foot to brow.
Now what else would you like to know?

RUMI

Where and When We Are

The real enemies of our life are the "oughts" and the "ifs." They pull us backward into the unalterable past and forward into the unpredictable future. But real life takes place in the here and the now. God is a God of the present. God is always in the moment, be that moment hard or easy, joyful or painful. When Jesus spoke about God, he always spoke about God as being where and when we are. "When you see me, you see God. When you hear me, you hear God." God is not someone who was or will be, but the One who is, and who is for me in the present moment. That's why Jesus came to wipe away the burden of the past and the worries for the future. He wants us to discover God right where we are, here and now.

HENRI J. M. NOUWEN

This is more simple than philosophy or religion. It is about not looking anywhere else but here.

Stop Pretending

The great teachings unanimously emphasize that all the peace, wisdom, and joy in the universe are already within us; we don't have to gain, develop, or attain them. Like a child standing in a beautiful park with his eyes shut tight, there's no need to imagine trees, flowers, deer, birds, and sky; we merely need to open our eyes and realize what is already here, who we already are—as soon as we stop pretending we're small or unholy.

I could characterize nearly any spiritual practice as simply being: identify and stop, identify and stop, identify and stop. Identify the myriad forms of limitation and delusion we place upon ourselves, and muster the courage to stop each one. Little by little deep inside us, the diamond shines, the eyes open, the dawn rises, we become what we already are. *Tat Twam Asi* (Thou Art That).

BO LOZOFF

Without the thought that you are insignificant or unenlightened, who are you? Now is the best time to stop pretending.

When you live with this awareness, there's no fretting about making this or that happen or go away. Take, for example, sitting up in bed in the morning, putting on socks, and applying the same awareness to putting on socks as you give to following your breath on your [meditation] cushion. There's just your arm moving, the feel of the sock pulling up over your foot, the arch of your neck as you bend over. Thinking of nothing at all, putting every bit of yourself into simply pulling on that sock. Suddenly the world opens up. There's an enormous rush of joy for no reason at all. Everything outside you and inside you is swallowed up by that sock going over your toes. It all happens so fast, you can't even say how long the moment lasts. There's not even any sense of you pulling on the sock. It could just as easily be the sock pulling you on. You and your sock and your foot and your elbow and your neck have somehow all vanished into the act itself. It's not that you physically disappear or go into some altered state; it's just that you've dropped into the pure joy of closing the gap between yourself and the moment of pulling on your sock.

MANFRED B. STEGER AND PERLE BESSERMAN

Where is the gap between yourself and the world? It closes in an instant. Did it ever exist? Put on your socks. See for yourself.

Opening from Heart

Right now, and in every now-moment, you are either closing or opening. You are either stressfully waiting for something—more money, security, affection—or you are living from your deep heart, opening as the entire moment, and giving what you most deeply desire to give, without waiting.

If you are waiting for *anything* in order to live and love without holding back, then you suffer. Every moment is the most important moment of your life. No future time is better than now to let down your guard and love.

Everything you do right now ripples outward and affects everyone. Your posture can shine your heart or transmit anxiety. Your breath can radiate love or muddy the room in depression. Your glance can awaken joy. Your words can inspire freedom. Your every act can open hearts and minds.

Opening from heart to all, you live as a gift to all. In every moment, you are either opening or closing. Right now, you are choosing to open and give fully or you are waiting. How does your choice feel?

DAVID DEIDA

How does it feel when you turn away from a stranger, a neighbor, a co-worker, or your thoughts and feelings? When you do this, notice how you reject nirvana showing up right now.

Enter the Fire

The only way to achieve maximum openness is to arrive at every moment without a single pre-conception. Otherwise, we resist what doesn't fit our model. Regardless of how much we know, or how evolved we've become, we must put every bit of that aside. We must step into the mystery naked and undefended.

When we truly hate what's happening, our instinct is to flee from it like a house on fire. But if we can learn to turn around and enter that fire, to let it burn all our resistance away, then we find ourselves arising from the ashes with a new sense of power and freedom.

Sometimes, without any answers to hold on to, it seems like we're nothing at all. Other times, overwhelmed by life's roaring torrent, it seems like we're everything at once. These two impressions are actually flipsides of the same coin. They're a taste of what happens when the barriers of our personality become porous. We encounter life directly, without anything to mediate its intensity. We see clearly, in those moments, how the self we carry with us is no more or less than a tool of our organism, a system that allows us to function, but that also, miraculously, we have the ability to step right through.

RAPHAEL CUSHNIR

Nothing Exists Outside the Now

Q: Aren't past and future just as real, sometimes even more real, than the present? After all, the past determines who we are, as well as how we perceive and behave in the present. And our future goals determine which actions we take in the present.

A: You haven't yet grasped the essence of what I am saying because you are trying to understand it mentally. The mind cannot understand this. Only *you* can. *Please just listen.* Have you ever experienced, done, thought, or felt anything outside the Now? Do you think you ever will? Is it possible for anything to happen or *be* outside the Now? The answer is obvious, is it not? Nothing ever happened in the past; it happened in the Now. Nothing will ever happen in the future; it will happen in the Now.

What you think of as past is a memory trace, stored in the mind, of a former Now. When you remember the past, you reactivate a memory trace—and you do so now. The future is an imagined Now, a projection of the mind. When the future comes, it comes as the Now. When you think about the future, you do it now. Past and future obviously have no reality of their own. Just as the moon has no light of its own, but can only reflect the light of the sun, so are the past and future only pale reflections of the light, power, and reality of the eternal present.

ECKHART TOLLE

Without the story of a past, who are you in this timeless present? Without a projection of an imagined future, who are you now?

The First Principle

"You talked about the first principle again, but I still don't know what it is," I said to Suzuki.

"I don't know," he said, "*is* the first principle."

SHUNRYU SUZUKI

Many times during the day, I say to myself, "I don't know." When I don't know, I see the world with fresh eyes, an openness Suzuki calls "beginner's mind." Now there are new possibilities. After all, what do I really know?

When You Follow the Mirage

So what is the point of waiting? What exactly are you waiting for? Is somebody going to give you what you always wanted? Will a train come from Heaven bringing you goodies? But nothing that could ever happen could be as good, as precious, as who you are.

What stops you from being, from being present, is nothing but your hope for the future. Hoping for something to be different keeps you looking for some future fantasy. But it is a mirage; you'll never get there. The mirage stops you from seeing the obvious, the preciousness of Being. It is a great distortion, a great misunderstanding of what will fulfill you. When you follow the mirage, you are rejecting yourself.

A. H. ALMAAS

What are you waiting for?

Y ou search for God through heaven and earth,
but you don't know the one who is right before
your eyes, because you don't know to search
into this very moment.

JESUS

What?

What would we have to
hold in compassion
to be at peace right now?

What would we have to
let go of
to be at peace right now?

JACK KORNFIELD

Peace is always here. Is there something standing
in your way?

Just being at the piano—egoless—is to reach the place where the only thing that exists is the sound and the moving toward the sound. The music on the page that was outside of you is now within you, and moves through you; you are a channel for the music, and play from the center of your being. Everything that you have consciously learned, all of your knowledge, emanates from within you. There is a sense of oneness in which the heart of the musician and the heart of the composer meet, in which there is no room for self-conscious thought. You are one with yourself and the act, and feel as if playing has already happened and you are effortlessly releasing it. The music is in your hands, in the air, in the room, the music is everywhere, and the whole universe is contained in the experience of playing.

MILDRED CHASE

When you become your activity, the "I" is forgotten. There is just music, and it is everywhere and everything.

Right Here, Right Now

I am ... the divine expression exactly as I am, right here, right now. You are the divine expression exactly as you are, right here, right now. It is the divine expression, exactly as it is, right here, right now. Nothing, absolutely nothing, needs to be added or taken away. Nothing is more valid or sacred than anything else. No conditions need to be fulfilled. The infinite is not somewhere else waiting for us to become worthy.

I do not have to experience "the dark night of the soul," or surrender, be purified, or go through any kind of change or process. How can the illusory separate self practice something in order to reveal that it is illusory? I don't need to be serious, honest, dishonest, moral or immoral, aesthetic or gross. There are no reference points. The life story that has apparently happened is uniquely and exactly appropriate for each awakening. All is just as it should be, right now. Not because it is a potential for something better, but simply because all that *is* is divine expression.

TONY PARSONS

This is a beautiful song of recognition. If you get caught up in seeking and striving, just sit still and read this out loud to yourself, as if it was written only for you.

Smack! into the Moment

Literature gives us the great gift of the present moment. As we read we enter the author's mind and follow it like a train on its tracks . . . She is taking us far out or far in and we're there!—no place else. Mind to mind . . .

But you ask, isn't the present moment just this: the sun coming in through the window, me leaning on a wooden desk, my eyes darting along the page, my legs crossed—not trucking along, my mind deep in the author's story?

Yes, that also is the present moment, but usually if I'm sitting there without reading, I am a divided person. Half of me is there, the other half is out the window, down the block shopping for wild rice, thinking about supper or how mad I am at a friend. But when I'm reading andI love what I'm reading, I'm totally connected, whole. Me and Shakespeare, me and Milton—no time or space between us. We are one—not two, not split. Then with that oneness, full of concentration and presence, I look up and can really see and experience through my whole body the light coming in through the glass pane and how it plays on the desktop where my book is, and I can feel my legs crossed underneath.

NATALIE GOLDBERG

Are you reading now, in full presence and connection?

Welcome Morning
(excerpt)

There is joy
in all:
in the hair I brush each morning,
in the Cannon towel, newly washed,
that I rub my body with each morning,
in the chapel of eggs I cook
each morning,
in the outcry from the kettle
that heats my coffee
each morning,
in the spoon and the chair
that cry "hello there, Anne"
each morning
in the godhead of the table
that I set my silver, plate, cup upon
each morning.
All this is God . . .

ANNE SEXTON

22

In
Your
Face

It is right in your face.
This moment,
the whole thing is handed to you.

YUANWU

Are you receiving "it" now?

Forget
Yourself

In that sense we can say that the purpose of (Zen) practice is no purpose. If we have a purpose, then we have problems. We set up all kinds of goals and we reach for them. But the amazing thing is that the goal is right here! We are on the starting line and at the same time we are already on the goal line. In other words, we are already living the buddhas' life. Regardless of whether we realize it or not, regardless of whether we are new or old-time practitioners, we are intrinsically the buddhas. Yet until we see this, somehow we simply cannot accept that fact.

, , , The most important point is to forget yourself. What we do most of the time is exactly the opposite. We reinforce the self. Always, *I* am doing something. This is the problem; we create this separation. When you truly forget yourself, a very different scenery is revealed in front of your nose. The other shore is where you stand. The buddhas' life is your life. So please, however you have been practicing, really focus on forgetting yourself.

TAIZAN MAEZUMI ROSHI

So, how exactly can you forget yourself? If you try to annihilate your ego, it won't work; self isn't an object that exists. Instead, simply notice your thoughts and feelings—question their truth.

What I'm leading you to is the following: awareness of the reality around you. Awareness means to watch, to observe what is going on within you and around you. "Going on" is pretty accurate: Trees, grass, flowers, animals, rock, *all* of reality is moving. One observes it, one watches it. How essential it is for the human being not just to observe himself or herself, but to watch all of reality. Are you imprisoned by your concepts? Do you want to break free of your prison? Then *look;* observe; spend hours observing. Watching what? *Anything.* The faces of people, the shapes of trees, a bird in flight, a pile of stones, watch the grass grow. Get in touch with things, look at them. Hopefully you will then break out of these rigid patterns we have all developed, out of what our thoughts and our words have imposed on us. Hopefully we will see. What will we see? This thing that we choose to call reality, whatever is beyond words and concepts. This is a *spiritual* exercise—connected with breaking out of your cage, out of the imprisonment of the concepts and words.

How sad if we pass through life and never see it with the eyes of a child . . .

ANTHONY DE MELLO

Without self-blame, return your attention to what is in front of your nose. When you do this as gently as possible, it becomes natural and spontaneous.

Where
I
Am

Wherever my travels may lead, paradise is where I am.

VOLTAIRE

Take off your shoes. The ground where you stand is holy ground.

EXODUS 1:5–6

This is life eternal. This, all that youth will give to you. It is the season for wine, roses and drunken friends. Be happy for this moment. This *moment* . . . is your life.

OMAR KHAYYAM

Earnestness is the key. Unconditional willingness. All you have to do is pay attention, be honest, and follow through. Truth is discovered when you simply refuse to lie to yourself anymore. Love is discovered when you stop indulging in self centeredness, fear, and anger. You don't have to improve yourself; just sort through the contradictions. Your desire is to love and be loved, yet you use and hurt and alienate the ones you wanted to love the most. You want to be honest, but you find a million excuses for continuing the pretense, for self righteousness, for psychological defense. You want to be happy and at peace, yet you cling to competitive, erroneous, and hurtful views of things.

Do you really want to be happy? Just pay attention and be kind, unconditionally kind, on this breath alone. Forget about the future. Just this breath. No matter what the circumstances, just be kind. Friend, lover, family member, someone who seems to hate you, someone you've never met on the street, your own soft animal body. Just be kind, in whatever way is appropriate. Everything else will work itself out, and you will begin to sense your own Pure Heart everywhere. How amazing.

Very simple. Just be kind.
Only on this breath.

SCOTT MORRISON

> Forget trying to have big compassionate thoughts. Be kind on this breath. Be kind to the one who breathes.

27

The Great Search

I n its highest form, the sensation of seeking takes on the form of the Great Search for Spirit. We wish to get from our unenlightened state (of sin or delusion or duality) to an enlightened or more spiritual state. We wish to get from where Spirit is not, to where Spirit is . . .

The Great Search for Spirit is simply that impulse, the final impulse, which prevents the present realization of Spirit, and it does so for a simple reason: the Great Search presumes the loss of God. The Great Search reinforces the mistaken belief that God is not present, and thus totally obscures the reality of God's ever-present Presence. The Great Search, which pretends to love God, is in fact the very mechanism of pushing God away; the mechanism of promising to find tomorrow that which exists only in the timeless now; the mechanism of watching the future so fervently that the present always passes it by—very quickly—and God's smiling face with it.

KEN WILBER

Lift the stone and you will find me; Cleave the wood and I am there.

JESUS

Face to face—all the time.

SHIYU

Isn't it funny?—I have been studying happiness for at least forty years, but I still don't have a definition of it. The closest one would be that happiness is the state of mind in which one does not desire to be in any other state. Being deeply involved in the moment, we do not have the opportunity to think about anything but the task at hand—hence, by default, we are happy.

MIHALY CSIKSZENTMIHALYI

Truth has no special time of its own. Its hour is now—always.

ALBERT SCHWEITZER

Inner Awareness

Most of us think that awareness is a mysterious something to be practiced, and that we should get together day after day to talk about awareness. You don't come to awareness that way at all. But if you are aware of outward things— the curve of a road, the shape of a tree, the color of another's clothes, the outline of the mountains against the blue sky, the delicacy of a flower, the pain on the face of a passer-by, the ignorance, the envy, the jealousy of others, the beauty of the earth— then, seeing all these outward things without condemnation, without choice, you can ride on the tide of inner awareness. Then you will become aware of your own reactions, of your own pettiness, of your own jealousies. From the outward awareness, you come to the inward; but if you are not aware of the outer, you cannot possibly come to the inner.

When there is inward awareness of every activity of your mind and your body, when you are aware of your thoughts, of your feelings, both secret and open, conscious and unconscious, then out of this awareness there comes a clarity that is not induced, not put together by the mind. And without that clarity, you may do what you will, you may search the heavens, and the earth, and the deeps, but you will never find out what is true.

J. KRISHNAMURTI

Y ou are not the mind. It is axiomatic that the perceiver cannot be the perceived. You can perceive your body; therefore, you are not the body. You can perceive your thoughts; therefore, you are not the mind. That which cannot be perceived or conceived is what you ARE.

If any individual considers himself enlightened, then he is not. The precondition of enlightenment is that the identified individual self has been annihilated. No personal self or individual phenomenon has *ever* been enlightened. The person disappears along with all other phenomena when he awakens from this dream of existence.

Self-Realization is effortless. What you are trying to find is what you *already are*. Enlightenment is total emptiness of mind. There is nothing you can do to get it. Any effort you make can only be an obstruction to it.

If you but cease from useless conceptualizing, you will be what you are and what you have always been. Seeing *truly* is not merely a change in the direction of seeing but a change in its very center, in which the seer himself disappears.

RAMESH S. BALSEKAR

Instead of trying to stop your judgments, practice the simplest form of awareness: notice your thoughts and beliefs as they arise and inquire into their truth.

A Moment of Nothing Special

[Maria Housden's three-year-old daughter, Hannah, was diagnosed with terminal cancer.]

It was right then that it happened. It was such a strange and glorious thing that if I hadn't experienced it myself, I wouldn't have believed it was possible. I forgot that Hannah was sick! I wasn't even aware of having forgotten. It was as if I had been sucked out of the story of cancer, treatment, worry, and death. Hannah was playing in the dirt, and I was visiting with a friend. It was a moment of nothing special, of nothing going on. In a flash, whatever had sucked me up spit me out again. Even so, something felt different. Although I remembered now that Hannah was sick, some part of the stillness had remained.

Later, I sat on the front porch, in the residue of that stillness, peeling away the layers of night sky . . . The night sky was like my life, each layer a level of experience. No element or moment of it was more or less, better or worse, than any other; each was an offering to the whole, in its suspended, inky stillness.

Listening to the night, I felt poised on the edge of greatness, certain that the silence I was feeling was God.

MARIA HOUSDEN

Preoccupations and concerns suddenly drop away, and in this moment, the vast OK-ness of everything shines through. The greatness of nothing special.

The Amusement Park

The present moment is always here; where are you? When you are not present, where exactly do you go?

In school, my teachers took roll call to see who was in class. We were expected to say "present." If we did not respond, we were thought to be elsewhere. If the teacher saw that we were in class but did not say present, the roll call stopped until we became present enough to say "present." Sometimes when I was in class, I didn't say "present." Where was I? I was in the amusement park of my mind. The mind is full of exciting rides. Some are fun. Some are scary. Others leave us in a sentimental mood. However, none of the rides are here, where the teacher is waiting.

The mind swings in great unstoppable arcs from the past to the future. The mind can never be present. The mind can only see the present in its rearview mirror, because the present is too real and immediate. For the mind, the present is just another idea, another concept. The mind creates representations of reality; it can never grasp reality because reality itself is too subtle. Only when we leave the amusement park of our mind can we enter reality.

ROBERT RABBIN

Beginning
of
the
String

There must be complete attention to the present moment, as this is the beginning of the string. In following it with complete attention, this string will lead ever inward; supporting ideas are uncovered in this discovery. If we are able to give *complete attention* to each step as it unfolds, thought is not trapped in duality and therefore there is no goal. Thought does not know what constitutes the "central core" of its being. As each idea is come upon in the following string of events, there is no knowing what the future holds. For all we know this may be the last thing to be totally seen through prior to awakening. Time, in one way, is not involved. If it is possible to follow anything right straight through to its end, no time is involved. It can happen immediately. It only takes time, chronologically speaking, when we are unable to follow straight through with complete attention. This is the origin of the idea that time is required. This idea of time gives rise to the false ideas of postponement, spiritual growth, progress, a Savior, Gurus, the Path, and reincarnation as the ultimate postponement. These are given as excuses for our own inadequacy, in not being able to follow one thing directly to the end. We may give a thousand reasons for this inability, but the stark facts remain. Becoming discouraged because of past mistakes also does not solve the problem. With each failure can come self-discovery with renewed energy.

ALBERT BLACKBURN

Endless Celebration

Life can never be bad. It's a contradiction in terms. Life is life. . . . We lie down and go to sleep and then wake up again. Did you ever realize that every day you woke up? To wake up every day . . . Every morning one comes into the world. There is no end to it . . . and things grow. The market's a medley of green lettuce, red cherries, golden grapes and purple eggplants . . . all the colors of the rainbow! It's extraordinary! Incredible! Like a fairy tale! And you breathe the air. You never realize you're breathing. You must think about it. Remember! I'm sure it never crosses your mind. It's a miracle! Some people can never understand! It's wonderful to feel bored and *not* to feel bored, too, to lose one's temper and *not* to lose one's temper, to be *dis*contented and to be content. To practice resignation and to insist on your rights. You get excited, you talk and people talk to you, you touch and they touch you. All this is magical, like some endless celebration.

EUGENE IONESCO

From Where We Are Standing

When we let go of wanting something else to happen in this moment, we are taking a profound step toward being able to encounter what is here now. If we hope to go anywhere or develop ourselves in any way, we can only step from where we are standing. If we don't really know where we are standing—a knowing that comes directly from the cultivation of mindfulness—we may only go in circles, for all our efforts and expectations. So, in meditation practice, the best way to get somewhere is to let go of trying to get anywhere at all.

JON KABAT-ZINN

We are always trying so hard to get somewhere. How would it feel to just stop all that effort and be still?

The Only Teacher

Wittgenstein claimed that philosophy left everything just as it found it. Philosophy doesn't create a new, more precise language to replace the one we already speak. Rather, it helps us to pay attention to what is already right in front of us and teaches us to examine how our language actually works. Zen, too, leaves everything alone. But for most of us, leaving things alone turns out to be hard work! Without the hard work, we don't seem to be able to leave our life alone and *just live*. Faced with the dilemma of suffering, consciously and unconsciously, we seek an antidote or an escape. And by seeking to escape our suffering we turn our life inside out, contorting our "ordinary mind" into an "isolated mind" that seeks to distance, control, and dissociate an inner "me" from outer pain. We chase after enlightenment or other special states of consciousness that will relieve all suffering and guarantee perfect happiness, or so we've heard. Whether our project is the flight from pain or the pursuit of happiness, the outcome is the same: a life in flight from itself and from this moment. And this moment turns out to be the only answer there is, the only self there is, the only teacher, and the only reality. All hidden in plain sight.

BARRY MAGID

Touching
Miracles

According to the Buddha, my teacher, life is only available in the here and now. The past is already gone, and the future is yet to come. There is only one moment for me to live—the present moment. So the first thing I do is to go back to the present moment. By doing so, I touch life deeply. My in-breath is life, my out-breath is life. Each step I take is life . . .

Many of us think that happiness is not possible in the present moment. Most of us believe that there are a few more conditions that need to be met before we can be happy. This is why we are sucked into the future and are not capable of being present in the here and now. This is why we step over many of the wonders of life. If we keep running away into the future, we cannot be in touch with the many wonders of life—we cannot be in the present moment where there is healing, transformation, and joy.

THICH NHAT HANH

When you find your thoughts preoccupied with future imaginings, there is no need to berate yourself. Gently notice that you are only here now.

[The direct way to become a Buddha] is no other than the realization of your own Mind. Now what is this mind? It is the true nature of all sentient beings, that which existed before our parents were born and hence before our own birth, and which presently exists, unchangeable and eternal. So, it is called one's Face before one's parents were born. This Mind is intrinsically pure. When we are born it is not newly created, and when we die it does not perish. It has no distinction of male or female, nor has it any coloration of good or bad. It cannot be compared with anything, so it is called Buddha-nature. Yet countless thoughts issue from this Self-nature as waves arise in the ocean or as images are reflected in a mirror.

To realize your own Mind you must first of all look into the source from which thoughts flow. Sleeping and working, standing and sitting, profoundly ask yourself, "What is my own Mind?" with an intense yearning to resolve this question. This is called "training" or "practice" or "desire for truth" or "thirst for realization." What is termed zazen (meditation) is no more than looking into one's own Mind.

BASSUI

Zen teaches that great questioning leads to great enlightenment. Here is your koan: at this moment, who is reading these words?

39

Not Hidden

A Hasid burst into the study of Reb Yerachmiel ben Yisrael. "Rebbe," he said breathlessly, "what is the way to God?"

The Rebbe looked up from his studies and answered, "There is no way to God, for God is not other than here and now."

"Then, Rebbe, tell me the essence of God."

"There is no essence of God, for God is all and nothing."

"Then, Rebbe, tell me the secret that I might know that God is all."

"My friend," Reb Yerachmiel sighed, "there is no way, there is no essence, there is no secret. The truth you seek is not hidden from you. You are hiding from it."

RABBI RAMI M. SHAPIRO

What truth are you hiding from? Right now.

"A fresh road, and fresh plans!" he (Zorba) cried. "I've stopped thinking all the time of what happened yesterday. And stopped asking myself what's going to happen tomorrow. What's happening today, this minute, that's what I care about. I say: 'What are you doing at this moment, Zorba?' 'I'm sleeping.' 'Well, sleep well.' 'What are you doing at this moment, Zorba?' 'I'm working.' 'Well, work well.' 'What are you doing at this moment, Zorba?' 'I'm kissing a woman.' 'Well, kiss her well, Zorba! And forget all the rest while you're doing it; there's nothing else on earth, only you and her! Get on with it!'"

NIKOS KAZANTZAKIS

Awareness Is All

Thought is always stepping into the picture as "me," the main character—damming up the stream of events with self-reference, reacting and commenting and emoting about "myself"—becoming attached to what is experienced and felt as "good me," and rejecting of what is judged as "bad me": "I don't want to be that way. This is not me. I don't like it." We are clinging, denying, or escaping from ourselves all the time.

Where are we right now? What are we? Is it possible to observe these ever-changing states of feelings and emotions dispassionately *without becoming the owner or disowner of any of them?*

Pure awareness is the essence of what we truly are. We are not the different states and feelings, moods and tempers succeeding one another. All of it comes and goes lightly, cloudlike, without leaving a trace, when thought doesn't identify with any of it. To be here now is just to see, just to hear, to experience it all like the plane humming [an airplane is flying overhead] without needing to become anything. All listening, without being a listener.

What am I, this very moment, without knowing?

TONI PACKER

The Buddha's realization of nirvana was actually a discovery of that which had been present all the time. The Buddha did not enter some new territory: he saw things the way they were. What was extinguished was only the *false view* of self. What had always been illusory was understood as such. Nothing was changed but the perspective of the observer. When asked, "What are you?" by an awestruck would-be follower, the Buddha responded only, "I am awake." As one important Mahayana Sutra put it, "If we are not hampered by our confused subjectivity, this our worldly life is an activity of Nirvana itself."

What Are You?

The Buddha's realization of nirvana was actually a discovery of that which had been present all the time. The Buddha did not enter some new territory: he saw things the way they were. What was extinguished was only the *false view* of self. What had always been illusory was understood as such. Nothing was changed but the perspective of the observer. When asked, "What are you?" by an awestruck would-be follower, the Buddha responded only, "I am awake." As one important Mahayana Sutra put it, "If we are not hampered by our confused subjectivity, this our worldly life is an activity of Nirvana itself."

MARK EPSTEIN

Your thought patterns and beliefs are stories that you've been telling for a lifetime. Storyteller, who are you? Without the stories, what are you?

The Heart of Wisdom

Form is no other than emptiness,

emptiness is no other than form;

Form is precisely emptiness,

emptiness precisely form;

Sensation, perception, reaction, and consciousness are also like this.

. . . all things are expressions of emptiness, not born, not destroyed.

Not stained, not pure; neither waxing, nor waning.

Thus emptiness is not form, not sensation, not perception, reaction nor consciousness;

No eye, ear, nose, tongue, body, mind;

No color, sound, smell, taste, touch, thing;

No realm of sight, no realm of consciousness;

No ignorance, no end to ignorance;

No old age and death, no cessation of old age and death;

No suffering, no cause or end to suffering, no path;

No wisdom and no gain.

No gain—thus;

Bodhisattvas live this Prajna Paramita

With no hindrance of mind—no hindrance therefore no fear

Far beyond all such delusion, Nirvana is already here.

HEART SUTRA

Recited daily in Zen temples, this text is regarded as ultimate nondual wisdom or "Prajna Paramita." There are no opposites. When this is seen, nirvana is seen.

Circumstance
(excerpt)

All of what i feel—and for all i know
there is no high—and there is no low

>   no standin' wave—no rollin' stone
>   no ramblin' man—no great unknown

and there is no time—and there is no place
and there is no form—and there is no face . . .
All of what i feel—and for all i see
there is no you—and there is no me

>   no howlin' wind—no drivin' rain
>   no fallin' star—no lonesome train

and there is no fountain—no river wide
no solid mountain—no crimson tide . . .
All of what i feel—and for all i am
there is no lion—and there is no lamb

>   no spinnin' wheel—no perfect square
>   no walkin' cane—no rockin' chair

and there is no how—and there is no when
and there is no now—and there is no then
and it's nothin' much—this endless sky . . .

BUTCH HANCOCK

Sacred Places

Within my body are all the sacred places of the world, and the most profound pilgrimage I can ever make is within my own body.

SARAHA

Closer is He than breathing
and nearer than hands and feet.

ALFRED, LORD TENNYSON

Spring comes with flowers, autumn with the moon,
summer with breezes and winter with snow.
When useless concepts don't stick in your mind,
this is your best season.

WU-MEN

When you come up to me, you leave the human region behind, you leave the living region behind, you leave the region of color and shape and materiality behind long before you get Here. Come all the way Here, and you leave everything behind. What am I Here? What is Here—this bare awareness of Being emerging from Non-being, the *I am* from the *I am not*—is where life comes from, is where everything comes from.

DOUGLAS E. HARDING

What Is There Now

When one perceives impermanence, the perception of no-self is established. With perception of no-self, the conceit of "I" is eliminated, and this is nirvana here and now.

THE BUDDHA

When the artificial "I" is left behind, the real "I" that remains perceives directly instead of through the refracting and muddy waters of the false "I." The "scent of the wild laurel," the "cypress tree in the courtyard," the cup of tea, the "when I'm hungry I eat, when I'm thirsty I drink, when I'm tired I lie down," the "nothing is hidden from you," of the Zen Masters are the straight-seeing. It is the water freed from the ice that held it frozen. But it is only looking straight out of your eyes, it is nothing far off, mysterious, out of touch, imperceptible at present: *it is what is there now.*

WEI WU WEI

Melt. Flow. Evaporate into the bright sky.

Don't Turn Your Head

Ring the bells that still can ring
Forget your perfect offering
There is a crack in everything
That's how the light gets in.

LEONARD COHEN

Don't turn your head. Keep looking
at the bandaged place. That's where
the light enters you.

And don't believe for a moment
that you're healing yourself.

RUMI

We're always trying to free ourselves from misery but we go about it the wrong way. There are a lot of small sweetnesses in life that we ignore because they're so fleeting. It's very important to look at what lifts our spirits and brings us happiness—to cherish those moments and cultivate appreciation. Happiness comes from being receptive to whatever arises rather than frantically trying to escape what's unpleasant.

PEMA CHÖDRÖN

Vision

Life moves on, whether we act as cowards or heroes. Life has no other discipline to impose, if we would but realize it, than to accept life unquestioningly. Everything we shut our eyes to, everything we run away from, everything we deny, denigrate or despise, serves to defeat us in the end. What seems nasty, painful, evil, can become a source of beauty, joy and strength, if faced with an open mind.

Every moment is a golden one for him who has the vision to recognize it as such.

HENRY MILLER

Have you ever been surfing? Imagine you're on your surfboard now, waiting for the big one to come. Get ready to get carried with that energy. Now, here it comes. Are you with that energy right now? That's empathy. No words—just being with that energy. When I connect with what's alive in another person, I have feelings similar to when I'm surfing.

To do this, you can bring in nothing from the past. So the more psychology you've studied, the harder it will be to empathize. The more you know the person, the harder it will be to empathize. Diagnoses and past experiences can instantly knock you off the board. This doesn't mean denying the past. Past experiences can stimulate what's alive in this moment. But are you present to what was alive *then* or what the person is feeling and needing in *this* moment?

If you think ahead to what to say next—like how to fix it or make the person feel better—BOOM! Off the board. You're into the future. Empathy requires staying with the energy that's here right now. Not using any technique. Just being present. When I have really connected to this energy, it's like I wasn't there. I call this "watching the magic show." In this presence, a very precious energy works through us that can heal anything, and this relieves me from my "fix-it" tendencies.

MARSHALL B. ROSENBERG, PHD

Secret Music

This world has no marks, signs or evidence of existence, nor the noises in it, like accident of wind or voices or heehawing animals, yet listen closely the eternal hush of silence goes on and on throughout all this, and has been going on, and will go on and on. This is because the world is nothing but a dream and is just thought of and the everlasting eternity pays no attention to it. At night under the moon, or in a quiet room, hush now, the secret music of the Unborn goes on and on, beyond conception, awake beyond existence. Properly speaking, awake is not really awake because the golden eternity never went to sleep: you can tell by the constant sound of Silence which cuts through this world like a magic diamond through the trick of your not realizing that your mind caused the world.

JACK KEROUAC

Right now, look straight at the present thought in your mind. Does it have a shape? Does it have a color? Did it ever really arise in the first place? Where does it abide? Where does it cease? When does it cease? Does it really cease? Did it come from anywhere? Does it go anywhere? When we cannot find any of these things, then we let go and rest at ease.

. . . When mind becomes distracted towards outer objects, we apply the instruction of the ship's captain and the crow. When the crow flies off the ship, just watch where it goes; you do not need to do anything else. However, upon examination, the thought that was distracted to outer objects is already gone, so there is nothing to look at. It is really awareness looking back at itself; thus, there is nothing to see, and there is no one looking. A bunch of crows can fly off in several directions at the same time, but thoughts are not like that. Thoughts are like paintings in water; they disappear as soon as you paint them. There is only mind looking at itself.

The main point is to look straight at whatever thought arises, and relax. This is known as the meditation method in which there is no difference between someone who is learned and someone who is not.

KHENPO TSULTRIM GYAMTSO

Look directly, now.

Forever

On my desk I have a tiny framed photo of my father, with his arm around me, standing next to a telescope at what is clearly a highway pull-off and vista point. The note on the back of the photo reads "Lookout Mountain, Windham, New York, July 12, 1939." So I am three years old. I know that he and I stood at many similar viewing scopes during my childhood, so I assume that my memory of his instruction for seeing clearly is a conflated one. I remember it as "Look with both eyes, Sylvia. Keep them open. And stand in front of the two lenses. Right here. Otherwise you won't see clearly."

Maybe this was the most important part: "Look *now*," my father would say, "because we'll have to leave soon, and you'll have missed it."

Here is the instruction: Only connect. Wherever you are, right now, pay attention. Forever.

SYLVIA BOORSTEIN

And don't forget—forever is always now.

If you give up hope, you will likely find your life is infinitely richer. Here's why: When you live in hope, it's usually because you're avoiding reality. If you hope your partner will stop drinking, aren't you really afraid he or she won't? Aren't you really afraid to take decisive action to change the situation? If you keep hoping the drinking will stop, you get to avoid the truly hard work of actually handling the situation effectively. Hope becomes a drug or soporific to get you through the pain a little longer. Like all drugs, it comes with side effects. One of the main side effects is that you become a little numb, a little less alive. Hoping a situation will change keeps you at a distance from your true feelings—sadness, anger, fear. Each of these feelings is best appreciated up close. Feel them deeply, and they will cease to bother you. Hope they'll go away, and they'll bother you all day.

GAY HENDRICKS

When hoping for something better to happen, how are you living in this moment?

Gratitude for Every Moment

[A husband cares for his wife as she dies from cancer.]

As in a dream, a great deal was happening continuously but instantaneously—as it were in the twinkling of an eye—within a context of changelessness. Huge meanings were palpable, but not graspable by the conscious mind. And as in a dream, I acted without reflection, without questioning. I found myself "living without a why"—repeating the same small tasks and gestures that a bedridden patient requires, always the same, always different. It was a life without discursive thought. As in a dream, too, it was difficult to concentrate, to focus in the usual way. And yet I found I gave my whole being, not just a part, to whatever activity was at hand.

To use another metaphor, time, each moment, became a gift, a grace. It was as if all rested in God's hands. Everything was given over and became gift. I no longer experienced the movement of time, the current of life, as horizontal—as having a before and after, a past and a future, the one in some sense behind, pushing, and the other ahead, approaching—but as vertical. Each moment came as a miraculous opportunity. A gift that was realized, received, in the giving back . . .

CHRISTOPHER BAMFORD

When nothing is avoided, everything is the face of what is.

56

Constant Magic

If our life lacks a constant magic, it is because we choose to observe our acts and lose ourselves in consideration of their imagined form instead of being compelled by their force.

ANTOIN ARTAUD

Here it is—right now.
Start thinking about it and you miss it.

HUANG PO

In Louisville, at the corner of Fourth and Walnut, in the center of the shopping district, I was suddenly overwhelmed with the realization that I loved all those people . . . even though we were total strangers. It was like waking from a dream of separateness.

. . . The whole illusion of a separate holy existence is a dream.

THOMAS MERTON

Nothing to Do

You can't seem to stop your mind from racing around everywhere seeking something. That's why the Patriarch said, "Hopeless fellows—using their heads to look for their heads!" You must right now turn your light around and shine it on yourselves, not go seeking somewhere else. Then you will understand that in body and mind you are no different than the patriarchs and Buddhas, and that there is nothing to do.

LIN-CHI (RINZAI)

Instead of trying to stop thoughts, just look directly into that which is aware of them. Shift attention from what is perceived as external and rest in wakefulness itself.

If you wish to be free,
Know you are the Self,
The witness of all these,
The heart of awareness.

Set your body aside.
Sit in your own awareness.

You will at once be happy,
Forever still,
Forever free.

Formless and free,
Beyond the reach of the senses,
The witness of all things.

So be happy!

Right or wrong,
Joy and sorrow,
These are of the mind only,
They are not yours.

You are everywhere,
Forever free.

THE HEART OF AWARENESS: ASHTAVAKRA GITA

Very Close to You

This teaching is not remote or mysterious.
It is not across the sea so (that you could say), "Who
will cross the sea and get it for us, so that we might
be able to hear it and keep it?"
It is very close to you.
It is in your mouth and in your heart
So that you can fulfill it.

DEUTERONOMY 30:11—14

The Old Testament vision of the world differs
from that of Eastern mysticism, but universal
insights like this are found in every tradition.

Driving Meditation

To practice Moving Meditation you must fully accept where you now find yourself, here in your car. Divest yourself of all expectations, standards of comparison and technique, take that clear, observing, unobstructed state of being, and keep on driving! Now, instead of sitting erect and attentive in a quiet stationary place like a zendo or meditation hall, you are now sitting erect and attentive in your moving vehicle. You are now meditating as you move along. Do not be ruled by anything inside or outside of you. See and experience without intrusion, but when an intrusion does rear its ugly head in the form of anger, an opinion, some driver cutting you off, simply acknowledge the stray image and return your focus to being aware of everything around you. Now, driving along, be intimately involved in the action and be aware that everything around you is happening for the first time. Everything is constantly changing, each traffic situation requiring its own set of responses. Nothing is left to rote. Keep your mind, body and senses wide awake, and as you drive along know that all that you see is as new as a baby's smile, no matter how many times you think you have seen it before.

K. T. BERGER

Try this. Spend an afternoon—walking, driving, eating—all experienced as if for the first time. Fresh, new, open.

The Precious Present

And then, it happened!
He didn't know why it happened
when it happened
It just . . . happened!

He realized that *The Precious
Present* was just that:

The Present

Not the past;
and not the future
but

The Precious Present.

He realized that
the present moment
is always precious.
Not because it is absolutely flawless,
which it often seems not to be.
But because it is
absolutely everything
it is meant to be . . .
at that moment.

SPENCER JOHNSON

We have all tried all kinds of meditation techniques. We are still conflicted, neurotic, unfulfilled.

We sit down exhausted from our efforts, dispirited. We throw out the whole idea of meditating. We give up.

And there we are. We have finally come to where we are. Where we are is meditation, wherever we are.

There is no entry and no exit. There is no doing and no not-doing. There is no technique, no result, no power, no experience.

The meditation of where we are is not even spiritual. It is life itself, moving of its own accord, fluid, quiet, beautiful, and self-fulfilled.

Where we are, there is no meditator, only meditation. There is no thinker, only thought. There is no doer, only action. There is no lover, only love.

We do not need a special time or place to be where we are. We do not need to retreat, to isolate, in order to be where we are. We do not need anything. We need nothing.

STEVEN HARRISON

Without a special time or place, what is meditation for you?

My Practice

Yes, I do have a personal practice. My practice is called "living human life" and I try to be regular in my practice. [We both laugh loudly.] Sometimes I forget my practice and start doing bizarre and strange things like meditating or holding my breath or something. But the practice that I am really committed to is living ordinary human life.

So my practice involves such *sadhana*[1] as being a parent to two beautiful boys. My *sadhana* involves having to listen when people notice things in me that are a little off and having to return to the humility of not being beyond reproach. My practice includes remembering to do things I said I would do. It includes being willing to be absolutely in the mud of humanity at the same time as being Consciousness. My practice has become to not use spiritual ideas, or fleeting spiritual experiences in any way whatsoever to avoid the curriculum of human life. . . .

I don't think that there is any need for any practice beyond just being here on this planet meeting what life brings you with an open heart.

ARJUNA NICK ARDAGH

Let's keep this simple. Be here. Be open.

[1]Sanskrit term meaning spiritual practice usually associated with "holy" activities.

To stay in the middle prepares us to meet the unknown without fear; it prepares us to face both our life and our death. The in-between state—where moment by moment the warrior finds himself learning to let go—is the perfect training ground. It really doesn't matter if we feel depressed about that or inspired. There is absolutely no way to do this just right . . .

As we continue to train, we evolve beyond the little me who continually seeks zones of comfort. We gradually discover that we are big enough to hold something that is neither lie nor truth, neither pure nor impure, neither bad nor good. But first we have to appreciate the richness of the groundless state and hang in there.

It's important to hear about this in-between state. Otherwise we think the warrior's journey is one way or the other; either we're all caught up or we're free. The fact is that we spend a long time in the middle. The juicy spot is a fruitful place to be. Resting here completely—steadfastly experiencing the clarity of the present moment—is called enlightenment.

PEMA CHÖDRÖN

The Buddha's middle way is the course of not clinging to any experience, state, or view. This is not arid philosophy but alive presence. This "in-between" holds on to nothing and rests nowhere.

Your Original Face

Hui-ming bowed [to Hui-neng, the Sixth Zen Patriarch] and said, "Please explain the teachings to me, Workman."[2]

I said, "Since you have come for the teaching, you should shut out all objects and not conceive a single thought; then I will expound the teaching for you."

Hui-ming was silent for a long while. I said, "When you do not think of good and do not think of bad, what is your original face?"

At these words, Hui-ming was greatly enlightened. Then he asked, "Is there any further secret idea besides the secret idea just now secretly spoken?"

I said, "What I have told you is no secret. If you reflect inwardly, the secret is in you."

HUI-NENG

If your original face is not what you see in the mirror nor the mask you show the world, then what is it?

[2]"Workman" refers to the Sixth Patriarch, who was a common laborer.

You Reading This, Be Ready

Starting here, what do you want to remember?
How sunlight creeps along a shining floor?
What scent of old wood hovers, what softened
sound from outside fills the air?

Will you ever bring a better gift for the world
than the breathing respect that you carry
wherever you go right now? Are you waiting
for time to show you some better thoughts?

When you turn around, starting here, lift this
new glimpse that you found; carry into evening
all that you want from this day. This interval you spent
reading or hearing this, keep it for life—

What can anyone give you greater than now,
starting here, right in this room, when you turn around?

WILLIAM STAFFORD

You already have the greatest gift. Turn around.

One with This

While sitting in meditation, and just after having said aloud for the benefit of his disciples, "No suppressing arrival, no following departure," [Zen Master] Daibai heard a weasel shriek, the "this" of the following poem. It is said that on reciting the poem, he indeed breathed his last.

I am one with this, this only.
You, my disciples,
Uphold it firmly.
Now I can breathe my last.

DAIBAI

As you read these words, you may hear a car passing or people talking. Be one with this. At this moment, there is no other. There is no next.

Giving Way to This

The river
where you set
your foot just now
is gone—
those waters
giving way to this,
now this.

HERACLITUS

Who Is in the Way?

Your letter informs me that your root nature is dim and dull, so that though you make efforts to cultivate and uphold [the Dharma], you've never gotten an instant of transcendent enlightenment. The one who can recognize dim and dull is definitely not dim and dull: where else do you want to seek transcendent enlightenment?

Just arouse yourself right here, and see what it is. The one who does the arousing isn't anyone else, he's just the one that can recognize dimness and dullness. And the one who recognizes dimness and dullness isn't anyone else, he's your own fundamental identity. This is me giving medicine to suit the disease, having no other alternative; briefly pointing out the road for you to return home and sit in peace, and that's all. . . .

Simply see what the one who can know dimness and dullness like this ultimately is. Just look right here, don't seek transcendent enlightenment. Just observe and observe, and suddenly you'll laugh aloud. Beyond this, there's nothing that can be said.

TA HUI

Right now, stop reading and simply notice how you are feeling. Take a deep breath. Rather than staying in the feeling, just step back. Observe the awareness that sees all of it.

I have realized that the past and future are real illusions, that they exist in the present, which is what there is and all there is.

ALAN WATTS

For the Now-moment, in which God made the first man and the Now-moment in which the last man will disappear, and the Now-moment in which I am speaking are all the one in God, in whom there is only one Now. Look! The person who lives in the light of God is conscious neither of time past nor of time to come but only of the one eternity.

MEISTER ECKHART

It's So Easy

Mind has inspired as much abstruse, one-hand-clapping discourse as any subject in Buddhism. Tenzin Palmo, however, says that there's no need to make a big fuss about it, because we experience mind whenever we see things as they really are: "If we can just stand still and let go, we've got pure awareness! It's so easy, because it's who we really are. . . ."

Tenzin Palmo doesn't care to hear any whining about the difficulty of getting in touch with mind. "We don't believe how simple it is, so we insist that it's hard," she says. "We don't need to do hours and hours of practice, but we don't believe that. We have to travel around the world to realize that we already have what we're looking for." She smiles and sighs. "It's very difficult for most people to realize that there's nothing to do."

WINIFRED GALLAGHER

Isn't life difficult enough? Why make it harder?
Stand still and see for yourself.

Spiritual people can be some of the most violent people you will ever meet. Mostly, they
are violent to themselves. They violently try
to control their minds, their emotions, and their bodies. They
become upset with themselves and beat themselves up for not
rising up to the conditioned mind's idea of what it believes
enlightenment to be. No one ever became free through such vio-
lence. Why is it that so few people are truly free? Because they
try to conform to ideas, concepts, and beliefs in their heads.
They try to concentrate their way to heaven. But Freedom is
about the natural state, the spontaneous and un-self-
conscious expression of beingness. If you want to find it, see
that the very idea of "a someone who is in control" is a concept
created by the mind. Take one step backward into the unknown.

ADYASHANTI

The "me" relentlessly moves forward in the hunt
for some imagined treasure. Do you have the
courage to take a step backward into the
unknown?

Now
Start
Living!

I would like you to break the habit of waiting. You have waited enough . . . you have already waited more than was needed. Now start living! And there is only one way to live and that is to start now! There is no tomorrow, the only time is now. All tomorrows are imaginary. The past is memory, the future is imagination. Only this moment is true and only this moment is the door to the divine.

. . . Immediately you will see a new life happening to you.

OSHO

Do you see it?

Just a Thought / Feeling Away

[Note: Dr. Taylor had a profound experience of nowness during a severe stroke.]

The stroke of insight has given me the priceless gift of knowing that deep inner peace is just a thought/feeling away. To experience peace does not mean that your life is always blissful. It means that you are capable of tapping into a blissful state of mind amidst the normal chaos of a hectic life. I realize that for many of us, the distance between our thinking mind and our compassionate heart sometimes feels miles apart. Some of us traverse this distance on command. Others of us are so committed to our hopelessness, anger and misery that the mere concept of a peaceful heart feels foreign and unsafe.

Based upon my experience with losing my left mind, I wholeheartedly believe that the feeling of deep inner peace is neurological circuitry located in our right brain. This circuitry is constantly running and always available for us to hook into. The feeling of peace is something that happens in the present moment. It's not something that we bring with us from the past or project into the future. Step one to experiencing inner peace is the willingness to be present in the right here, right now.

JILL BOLTE TAYLOR, PHD

Present
Wakefulness

Allow your present wakefulness to simply be;
Totally without fabrication.
Don't try to improve upon its freshness.
Remain unoccupied
By any memory of the past,
Any plan about the future;
Involved in any dualistic appreciation of the present.
Don't dwell upon anything as the object of meditation.
Remain totally free,
Vividly clear,
Wide awake.

TSOKNYI RINPOCHE

Natural awareness does not need any enhancement. What would it be like to stop trying to manipulate your mind and just be here?

Just One Time

Where you are going
and the place you stay
come to the same thing.
What you long for
and what you've left behind
are as useless as your name.
Just one time, walk out
into the field and look
at the towering oak—
an acorn still beating at its heart.

PETER LEVITT

Life
Itself

The danger, then, is that we can become so pre-occupied with the path that we do not go anywhere on it while all around us life goes on its way. [Meister] Eckhart concludes . . . that, "whoever seeks God without any special Way, finds Him as He really is . . . and He is life itself." But how can we seek God without having a special way to do it?

This brings us to a paradox compact as stone: Without a spiritual discipline we go nowhere, but a discipline intentionally followed may lead us only to the practice of the discipline.

It may well be that the key to this paradox lies in Eckhart's stark claim that what we are to seek is "life itself." If the disciplined life is something other than ordinary life, is it possible there is a discipline already hidden in the ordinary? Have we always been on our way towards being who we are before we were—without knowing it? Are we mystics before we try to be mystics, even before we know anything of mysticism?

As the Buddhists put it, we are all unaware Buddhas whose efforts to lift ourselves out of the ordinary hide our true natures from ourselves. . . .

JAMES P. CARSE

What is concentration:
Food in bowl, drink in glass.

DAVID ROTHENBERG

I came to realize clearly that mind is no other
than mountains, rivers, and the great wide
earth, the sun and the moon and the stars.

DOGEN

Nothing Was Wanting

We had a remarkable sunset one day last November. I was walking in a meadow, the source of a small brook, when the sun at last, just before setting, after a cold gray day, reached a clear stratum in the horizon, and the softest brightest sunlight fell on the dry grass and on the stems of the trees in the opposite horizon and on the leaves of the shrub-oaks on the hill-side, while our shadows stretched long over the meadow eastward, as if we were the only motes in its beams. It was such a light as we could not have imagined a moment before, and the air also was so warm and serene that nothing was wanting to make a paradise of that meadow. When we reflected that this was not a solitary phenomenon, never to happen again, but that it would happen forever and ever an infinite number of evenings, and cheer and reassure the latest child that walked there, it was more glorious still.

HENRY DAVID THOREAU

Begin to search and dig in thine own field
for this pearl of eternity that lies in it.
It cannot cost thee too much
nor canst thou buy it too dear,
for it is all.
And when thou hast found it,
thou wilt know that
all thou has sold or given away for it
is a mere nothing
as a bubble upon the water.

WILLIAM LAW

On the Subway

I was sitting alone on the downtown IRT [New York subway] on my way to pick up the children at their after-school music classes. The train had just pulled out of the Twenty-third Street station and was accelerating to its cruising speed. . . .

Then suddenly, the dull light in the car began to shine with exceptional lucidity until everything around me was glowing with an indescribable aura, and I saw in the row of motley passengers opposite the miraculous connection of all living beings. Not felt; saw. What began as a desultory thought grew into a vision, larger and unifying, in which all the people in the car hurtling downtown together, including myself, like all the people on the planet hurtling together around the sun—our entire living cohort—formed one united family, indissolubly connected by the rare and mysterious accident of life. No matter what our countless superficial differences, we were equal, we were one, by virtue of simply being alive at this moment out of all the possible moments stretching endlessly back and ahead. The vision filled me with overwhelming love for the entire human race and a feeling that no matter how incomplete or damaged our lives, we were surpassingly lucky to be alive. Then the train pulled into the station and I got off.

ALIX KATES SHULMAN

Wherever you are *is* the sacred place.

Nothing to It

Look inward at your own mind!
It seems quite exciting, when not examined.
But when examined, there is nothing to it.
Appearing without being, it is nothing but empty.
It cannot be identified saying, "That's it!"
But is evanescent and elusive like mist.

Look at whatever may appear
In any of the ten directions.
No matter how it may appear,
The thing in itself, its very nature,
Is the sky-like nature of mind,
Beyond the projection and dissolution of thought and concept.

Everything has the nature of being empty.
When the empty looks at the empty,
Who is there to look at something empty?

NYOSHUL KHENPO

Mind is empty—like space. Seek a special state
or experience and you miss it.

Round
and
Full

[Blinded as a child, Lusseyran grew up and joined the French Resistance. He was caught and imprisoned in a prisoner-of-war camp, where he became an inspiration to fellow prisoners.]

The remarkable thing was that listening to the fears of others had ended by freeing me almost completely from anxiety. I had become cheerful, and was cheerful almost all of the time, without willing it, without even thinking about it. . . .

How well I remember that September night when fifteen hundred Ukrainians set me down in the middle of their block, made a ring around me, sang, danced, played the accordion, wept, sang again—all this gravely and affectionately without ever shouting—that night I promise you I no longer needed to defend myself against the past or the future. The present was as round and full as a sphere and it warmed me many times over.

And finally, as for those men who were laughing and putting their arms around each other—for they were laughing within an hour—if anyone had told them that they were unhappy, that they were in a concentration camp, they would not have believed him. They would have chased him away.

JACQUES LUSSEYRAN

O﬩ne day an old man was circumambulating Reting Monastery. Geshe Drom said to him: "Sir, I am happy to see you circumambulating, but wouldn't you prefer to be practicing the dharma?"

Thinking this over, the old man felt he'd better cover himself by reading some Buddhist scriptures. While he was reading in the temple courtyard, Geshe Drom said, "I am happy to see you reading the dharma, but wouldn't you prefer to be practicing it?"

At this, the old man thought that the best way to cover himself would be to meditate single pointedly. He put aside his reading and sat on a cushion, his eyes half-closed. Drom said: "Good to see you meditating, but wouldn't you rather be practicing the dharma?"

With nothing else left to do, the old man asked: "Gesha-la, please, how should I practice the dharma?"

"When you practice," Drom replied, "there is no distinction between the dharma and your own mind."

TSUN BA JE GOM

Your mind is not separate from what you seek.

Everywhere at the Same Time

"Yes, Siddhartha," he said. "Is this what you mean? That the river is everywhere at the same time, at the source and at the mouth, at the waterfalls, at the ferry, at the current, in the ocean and in the mountains, everywhere, and that the present only exists for it, not the shadow of the past, nor the shadow of the future?"

"That it is," said Siddhartha, "and when I learned that, I reviewed my life and it was also a river, and Siddhartha the boy, Siddhartha the mature man, and Siddhartha the old man were only separated by shadows, not through reality. Siddhartha's previous lives were also not in the past, and his death and his return to Brahma are not in the future. Nothing was, nothing will be, everything has reality and presence.

HERMANN HESSE

Forget the Point

So the secret is just to say "Yes!" and jump off from here. Then there is no problem. It means to be yourself in the present moment, always yourself, without sticking to an old self. You forget all about yourself and are refreshed. You are a new self, and before that self becomes an old self, you say "Yes!" and you walk to the kitchen for breakfast. So the point of each moment is to forget the point and extend your practice.

SHUNRYU SUZUKI

Can you be so busy saying "Yes!" that there isn't time to say, "No"?

As
If

In due course, we shall come back to the starting point. Time cannot take us out of time, as space cannot take us out of space. All you get by waiting is more waiting. Absolute perfection is here and now, not in some future, near or far. The secret is in action—here and now. It is your behavior that binds you to yourself. Disregard whatever you think yourself to be and act as if you were absolutely perfect—whatever your idea of perfection may be. All you need is courage.

My grace is telling you now: look within. All you need you have. Use it. Behave as best you know, do what you think you should. Don't be afraid of mistakes; you can always correct them, only intentions matter. The shape things take is not within your power; the motives of your actions are.

SRI NISARGADATTA MAHARAJ

Here is an assignment. Live this day as if you are absolutely perfect, without fear or reservation.

Out
of the
Mouths
of a
Thousand
Birds
(excerpt)

There is the Prayer Call rising up like the sun out of the mouths of a thousand birds.

There is an astonishing vastness of movement and Life emanating sound and light from my folded hands and my even quieter simple being and heart.

My dear, is it true that your mind is sometimes like a battering ram running all through the city, shouting so madly inside and out about the ten thousand things that do not matter?

Hafiz, too, for many years beat his head in youth and thought himself at a great distance, far from an armistice with God.

But that is why this scarred old pilgrim has now become such a sweet rare vintage who weeps and sings for you. This is why Hafiz will forever in his verse play his cymbal and call to you.

O listen—listen more carefully to what is inside of you right now.

In my world, all that remains is the wondrous call to dance and prayer rising up like a thousand suns out of the mouth of a single bird.

HAFIZ

Nothing
to
Say

Birth, old age,
Sickness, and death:
From the beginning,
This is the way
Things have always been.
Any thought
Of release from this life
Will wrap you only more tightly
In its snares.
The sleeping person
Looks for a Buddha,
The troubled person
Turns towards meditation,
But the one who knows
That there's nothing to seek
Knows too that there's nothing to say.
She keeps her mouth closed.

LY NGOC KIEU[3]

[3]From *Women in Praise of the Sacred*, edited by Jane Hirshfield.

One day Maurine Stuart Roshi[4] was having tea with friends at her home in Cambridge when the telephone rang.

"Do Buddhas wear toe-nail polish?" a seven-year-old caller wanted to know.

"Are *you* wearing toe-nail polish?" Roshi responded.

"YES!" shouted the little girl, and hung up.

MAURINE STUART

Right now a moment of time is fleeting by! Capture its reality in paint! To do that we must put all else out of our minds. We must become that moment, make ourselves a sensitive recording plate . . . Give the image of what we actually see, forgetting everything that has been seen before our time.

PAUL CEZANNE

---

[4]*Roshi* is a Zen title meaning teacher or master.

When We Live It

We do not see that our life right here, right now is nirvana. Maybe we think that nirvana is a place where there are no problems, no more delusions. Maybe we think nirvana is something very beautiful, something unattainable. We always think nirvana is something very different from our own life. But we must really understand that it is right here, right now.

How is that possible? We can say that our practice is to close the gap between what we *think* our life is and our actual life as the subtle mind of nirvana. Or more to the point, how can we realize that there is really no gap to begin with?

Do not be dualistic. Truly be one with your life as the subtle mind of nirvana. That is what *subtle* means. Something is subtle not because it is hidden, nor because it is elusive, but because it is right here. We don't see it precisely because it is right in front of us. In fact, we are living it. When we live it, we don't think about it. The minute we think about it, we are functioning in the dualistic state and don't see what our life is.

TAIZAN MAEZUMI ROSHI

I spent years trying to build imaginary bridges between here and there. Then I saw that I had always been where I wanted to be. The only gap was in my perception.

Is there effort required on this path? Personally I find I have less and less energy to make an effort in any direction.

You can't make an effort without tension. But why do you make an effort? Only because you're looking for some result, for something outside yourself. Once you really know that what you're looking for is your real nature, you lose the impetus to strive. So first, see how you are constantly making an effort. As soon as you are aware of this process, you are already outside it. And it may come as an original perception that you are really stillness.

But doesn't even seeing this require some effort?

No. This seeing is your natural state. Just be aware that you *don't* see. Become more aware that you constantly react. Seeing requires no effort because your nature is seeing, is being stillness. The moment you're not looking for a result, not looking to criticize, to evaluate or conclude, just looking, then you can perceive this reacting, and you're no longer an accomplice to it.

JEAN KLEIN

Notice how effort operates in your life and the ways you strive for results. What are you seeking? Where do you think you're going?

There
Is
No
Next

In Zen meditation, there is no next.

OLD ZEN SAYING

Eternally and always there is only now, one and the same now; the present is the only thing that has no end.

ERWIN SCHRODINGER

List consciousness is a state of mind that is entirely future-oriented. With subtle but constant quality of rushing, it operates on the premise that life will happen once everything is crossed off the List. . . . When you are in list consciousness, you are leaning into the future and completely missing the present. Practicing presence punctures the fantasy that somehow life will begin when the kids' soccer season is over or when I lose ten pounds or even when I take that meditation course and learn how to be more present! Practicing presence is bringing ourselves to the recognition that life is happening right *now*—and it is inviting us to wake up and notice.

ABBY SEIXAS

The next time you are doing something absolutely ordinary, or even better the next time you are doing something absolutely *necessary*, such as pissing, or making love, or shaving, or washing the dishes or the baby or yourself or the room, say to yourself:

"So it's all come to this!"

LEW WELCH

It all comes to this. Reading these words. Look no further. Right in front of you. Just this.

Here
Is
His
Dwelling

You are seeking God, dear sister, and he is everywhere. Everything proclaims him to you, everything reveals him to you, everything brings him to you. He is by your side, over you, around and in you. Here is his dwelling and yet you still seek him. Ah! You are searching for God, the idea of God in his essential being. You seek perfection, and it lies in everything that happens to you—your suffering, your actions, your impulses are the mysteries under which God reveals himself to you. But he will never disclose himself in the shape of that exalted image to which you so vainly cling.

The present moment holds infinite riches beyond your wildest dreams but you will only enjoy them to the extent of your faith and love. The more a soul loves, the more it longs, the more it hopes, the more it finds. The will of God is manifest in each moment, an immense ocean which the heart only fathoms in so far as it overflows with faith, trust and love.

JEAN-PIERRE DE CAUSSADE

I invite you to drop your exalted images, holy ideas, and spiritual concepts. Return to this moment. This is the God you seek.

So again, how does one investigate? First, find out if there is anything that you believe you are, *anything* that is not simply a thought or a mental image, with accompanying emotional and physical sensations. If, upon careful examination, it becomes clear that everything you think about yourself, your entire identity, is nothing but the play of memory—things you have read or heard and thought about "your self," then it should also be clear that "you" does not exist . . .

Experimentally, if you like, for at least a few seconds, even give up on the idea that you *can exist.* If you do, you will discover what is *always here,* what has never been born and never dies. And you will discover that it has no limits. The invitation is to relax into it. To completely give up on all stories about it. To realize that there is no way to describe or contain it.

How could you be separate from that? You *are* that. There is just vast, infinite, everything. It is what you are. You are infinite, unconditional silence into which everything arises and disappears. So why not put an end to the game, the struggle, the pretense? Why not relax into not knowing? It is absolute, unconditional peace and absolute, unconditional safety. Relax into what you are.

SCOTT MORRISON

A Special Way of Looking

What we have been saying here is to forget about *all* goals; in fact, we have been emphasizing this very same point, excessively so almost. We have been saying there are no do's and don'ts . . . there are no guidelines. You must totally forget any other state that might be attainable. Just look at and concentrate on what is here and now. Once you do that, which is following a one hundred percent negative approach, you immediately begin to discover how you function and create misery for yourself. Upon seeing this clearly, something else falls into place all by itself. *You* don't do it; the whole process that is continually taking place within us is in thought. Thought is always striving to reach some delightful state. It wants gratification to itself. All the time, trying to attain, it is in conflict. So when you look at things with or through thought . . . you will ever be defeated, because thought will translate what it sees according to its own conditioning. . . .

So to look at one's thought process requires a special way of looking. It needs looking without a background—that is, the entire thought mechanism, which is always saying: this is good, this is bad, always deceiving itself, must be inactivated . . . When the observer and the observed are one, then that is an entirely different kind of seeing.

ROBERT POWELL

You don't need to add any prefabricated truth. Just subtract everything that's false. What remains?

Tasting Oatmeal

It was the second morning of weekend *sesshin* (retreat). All day the first day I sat through restlessness, pain, and boredom and wondered what I was doing here. What kept me sitting through this? When the second morning arrived, I couldn't imagine how I could go on.

We received breakfast seated on our cushions. When the meal server came, I held out my bowl. He placed some oatmeal in it. After everyone was served, we all ate together. I put a little oatmeal in my mouth and shivered. I was stunned, it was so completely delicious. I started to cry. In that moment I realized that no matter how many bowls I had eaten, I have never tasted oatmeal before.

ZEN STUDENT[5]

When we give up the idea that we know, we are often stunned by what is, and life is delicious.

[5]From *Zen Miracles* by Brenda Shoshanna.

Who Has Ever Defiled You?

A monk asked, "How does one get emancipated?"

The Master said, "Who has ever put you in bondage?"

Monk: "What is the Pure Land?"[6]

Master: "Who has ever defiled you?"

Monk: "What is nirvana?"

Master: "Who has ever subjected you to birth-and-death?"

SHI TOU

Who has ever put you in bondage?

---

[6]Pure Land—In Mahayana Buddhism, a cosmic or ideal realm established by a Buddha that is outside the worlds of suffering.

If I chase it, I separate into the chaser and the chased.

If I am it, I am it and nothing else.

JOHN LILLY

You do not need to leave your room. Remain sitting at your table and listen. Do not even listen, simply wait. Do not even wait, be quite still and solitary. The world will freely offer itself to you unmasked, it has no choice, it will roll in ecstasy at your feet.

FRANZ KAFKA

Real
Meditation

Real meditation is spontaneous. It is pure welcoming, because there is no choosing of whatever appears in the field of consciousness. There is no selection. There is only choiceless allowing, be it of external perceptions, feelings, bodily sensations, thoughts, or their absence. Everything is equally allowed to come into existence, not as a practice, but because the mind has understood its own limitations. That is all the truth-seeker needs to do. No further spiritual practice needs to be undertaken.

In this openness we live in the now. There is nothing to gain, nothing to lose. Awareness is not something to be acquired at the end of a process. We already have all we need.

FRANCIS LUCILLE

For years, as a Zen meditator, I prayed for a mystical ray gun that could zap away every negative thought. Then I discovered that thoughts weren't the enemy, and I learned to welcome them with open arms.

Tilicho
Lake

In this high place
it is as simple as this,
leave everything you know behind.

Step toward the cold surface,
say the old prayer of rough love
and open both arms.

Those who come with empty hands
will stare into the lake astonished,
there, in the cold light
reflecting pure snow

the true shape of your own face.

DAVID WHYTE

All That Is Real

O ne Tuesday in March, with about half of the shopping finished, I was standing at the super-market meat counter looking at a T-bone steak when, suddenly, I *became* the steak! And that's *all* that I was—a butchered animal lodged in a cold meat counter, ready to be bought, cooked, and eaten. I did not see myself from the outside as such, but from the inside, I felt my being intersperse with each molecule of the steak, each space between the molecules. Then, bound into that form, I felt suffocated in a dark pool of mud. I was lost inside this strange dimension of matter until something, a *feeling* of sorts, reminded me of myself. I desperately wanted to be *me* again, but there was a huge force opposing my return. . . .

Stupefied, I could not move, think, feel or hear. Everything stopped at that moment. All was still as I felt my feet merge with the floor. Then out of the silence, I began to hear something—not words, but a feeling-sound whose meaning I had to translate. My attention was completely focused on this message, which I knew could help me return to reality, yet it was outside my grasp. "What is it I need to know?" I pleaded silently. "Tell me!" Then I focused on my body, my breath. As the rustling sounds of paper bags fell upon my ears, the answer came: "Now is all that is real."

DONNA LEE GORRELL

Be Alive

You are seeing everything for the last time, and everything you see is gilded with goodbyes. The child's hand like a starfish on the pillow, your hand on the doorknob . . . It is the room where for years Christmases have happened, snow falling so thick by the window that sometimes it has started to snow in the room, brightness falling on tables, books, chairs, the gaudy tree in the corner, a family sitting there, snowmen, snowbound, snow blind to the crazy passing of what they think will never pass. And today now everything will pass because it is the last day. For the last time you are seeing this rain fall and in your mind that snow, this child asleep, this cat. For the last time you are hearing this house come alive because you who are part of its life have come alive. All the unkept promises if they are ever to be kept have to be kept today. All the unspoken words if you do not speak them today will never be spoken. The people, the ones you love and the ones who bore you to death, all the life you have in you to live with them, if you do not live it with them today will never be lived. . . .

Be alive if you can all through this day today of your life. . . .

FREDERICK BUECHNER

Were you planning to wait for tomorrow to be alive?

What Is Life for You?

Where are you looking for your life? What makes you feel most alive? What is life to you? Ponder these questions and enjoy them.

Now today, moment by moment, realize that each person and event that happens is life for you. Life is not somewhere else. See how fully you can accept the life that presents itself to you now.

BRENDA SHOSHANNA

People often say, "Life is passing me by." How is this possible with life always unfolding in this precise instant?

No Degrees

It is completely senseless to think about what comes after death, about heaven, paradise. It is not necessary to ask questions about what we become after this life. Such questions are the fruit of egoism, and torment people unnecessarily.

Here-and-now contains eternity.

To practice zazen[7] here and now is to practice the true teaching of the Buddha. There are no degrees or steps, zazen itself is satori,[8] here and now we are Buddha.

TAISEN DESHIMARU

---

[7]*Zazen*—seated Zen meditation.
[8]*Satori*—enlightenment experience.

The Meaning of Life

Q: Katie, I believe that life is meaningless. That's my experience. I can't find any meaning.

Katie: So, life is meaningless. Is that true?

Q: I just can't feel any meaning. That's the way it feels.

Katie: Is that true? Life is totally meaningful for me.

Q: Yeah, but not for me.

Katie: The meaning of life for me is to simply sit here with you. It never gets more complicated than that. It's just so close that you don't recognize it. What is the meaning of life? For me, it's to sit here. That's it. To sit. Until I walk. It's pretty simple stuff. What is life's purpose? To sit here with you.

BYRON KATIE

Can you drop your search for life's meaning and see that it is right in front of your nose?

Do not wait expectantly for a later day to become enlightened. You just must stir yourselves and turn [inward] to your own square inch [of mind]. Search there and do not seek elsewhere. If you do such a thing, hundreds of thousands of teachings and boundless matters concerning the Buddhas will all flow out of this and fill heaven and earth. It is important to avoid seeking the Way [externally]; it is nothing but trusting the Self.

Fetching and carrying away for countless eons, never for an instant being apart from the Self, still, if you do not know of its existence, you are like someone bearing it in their hands and looking for it east and west. However much confusion this may seem to be, it is nothing but forgetting the Self. Today, when we see it fully, the wonderful way of the Buddhas and the separate transmission of the patriarchal teachers consist in only this, so never doubt it.

KEIZAN

Keizan, the co-founder of the Soto Zen school in Japan, taught that just sitting in meditation was itself enlightenment. No seeking any special experience. Just sitting still.

A
Natural
Occurrence

Just a moment or two ago I was "washing my face." The sleeves of my jacket were getting in the way, my eyes were burning from the soap, and I thought "what a pain in the ass this is."

At that moment I realized I could stop resisting and allow the body to wash its own face. The illusion creating the resistance was that "I am washing my face," the "me" doing the washing was interfering with the process, not performing it. "I" was getting in the way of a natural occurrence.

Immediately upon releasing the illusion of control, the face was washed and dried without further trouble. No time seemed to pass from the moment "control" was released until the act was finished, and no burning of the eyes, no problem with the jacket sleeves, an instantaneous "act" occurred. It seems the body "knows" better how to clean itself than "I" do.

OMKARA DATTA

Alive and Kicking

Most people think that we live in the actual world while we are alive, and that after we take the last breath we somehow wander into a vague realm of the spirit. It is a great mistake to see two separate realms. Instead, where we live is in fact the spiritual realm, a realm of many billion worlds, which goes beyond three, four, or even infinite dimensions. Then, the danger is that we might think that this is a realm that is empty and boundless. Watch out! It's all manifested right here at this moment. It is alive and kicking.

SOEN NAKAGAWA

The kingdom of heaven is not only in your hands, it *is* your hands.

The Indweller

Q: Am I on the right track to the Source?

A: Still you have a doubt. You need a track to move from one place to another, just as you need a track to come from Malaysia to India. But in Realizing the Self, how many miles do you have to travel? To reach your Self, which way will you go? Do you need an airplane or a train or a car? You don't need any vehicle because what you search is right Now Here. This you must understand Now itself! Simply understand it and do not work for it. Understand that the Self is eternal and always Here! When you move from Here to anywhere the Self is not moving. Self is always within you and you move about. Self is the indweller in the heart. It indwells the heart cave. It is not mobile and everything exists in it. This you must get right now.

H. W. L. POONJA (POONJAJI)

The search for the exotic, the strange, the unusual, the uncommon has often taken the form of pilgrimages, of turning away from the world, the "Journey to the East," to another country or to a different religion. The great lesson from the true mystics, from the Zen monks, and now also from the Humanistic and Transpersonal psychologists—that the sacred is *in* the ordinary, that it is to be found in one's daily life, in one's neighbors, friends, and family, in one's own back yard, and that travel may be a *flight* from confronting the sacred—this lesson can be easily lost. To be looking elsewhere for miracles is to me a sure sign of ignorance that *everything* is miraculous.

ABRAHAM H. MASLOW

Here's another exercise: walk around today saying to yourself a few times per hour, "This is miraculous." No matter what is happening, say this. Just notice how this outlook changes how you relate to the everyday experiences.

One Single Koan

True meditation is making everything—coughing, swallowing, waving, movement and stillness, speaking and acting, good and evil, fame and shame, loss and gain, right and wrong—into one single koan.

HAKUIN

And you don't need to wait for a Zen Master to give this koan to you.

Friend, hope for the Guest while you are alive,
Jump into experience while you are alive!
Think . . . and think . . . while you are alive.
What you call "salvation" belongs to the time before
death.

If you don't break your ropes while you're alive,
do you think
ghosts will do it after?

The idea that the soul will join with the ecstatic
just because the body is rotten—
that is all fantasy.
What is found now is found then.
If you find nothing now,
you will simply end up with an apartment in the City of Death.
If you make love with the divine now, in the next life you will
have the face of satisfied desire.

KABIR

The idea that death brings liberation is another
concept that only creates more waiting. If you
want to meet the divine "guest," break your
ropes now.

The Time Is Now!

Salvation is now. We have a tendency to point ourselves backward or forward in time, but the Gospels say either we are letting Jesus save us now or we aren't letting him save us at all. It's called the always-available grace of the present moment.

But it's the first word Jesus preaches: "The time is now! The kingdom is present and here. Turn around. Believe the Good News." In these four phrases we have the summation of all of Jesus' teaching. It's nothing esoteric or pseudo-mystical, just the infinite nature of now.

RICHARD ROHR

The Source of Milk

Don't look for it outside yourself.
You are the source of milk. Don't milk others!

There is a milk fountain inside you.
Don't walk around with an empty bucket.

You have a channel into the ocean, and yet
You ask for water from a little pool.

Beg for that love expansion. Meditate only
on THAT. The Qur'an says,
And He is with you.

RUMI

Here and Now, Boys

There was a rustling in the bushes on his left and suddenly, like a cuckoo from a nursery clock, out popped a large black bird, the size of a jackdaw—only, needless to say, it wasn't a jackdaw. It clapped a pair of white-tipped wings and, darting across the intervening space, settled on the lowest branch of a small dead tree, not twenty feet from where Will was lying. Its beak, he noticed, was orange, and it had a bald yellow patch under each eye, with canary-colored wattles that covered the sides and back of its head with a thick wig of naked flesh. The bird cocked its head and looked at him first with the right eye, then with the left. After which it opened its orange bill, whistled ten or twelve notes of a little air in the pentatonic scale, made a noise like somebody having hiccups, and then, in chanting phrase, *do do sol do,* said, "Here and now, boys; here and now, boys."

The words pressed a trigger, and all of a sudden, he remembered everything. . . .

ALDOUS HUXLEY

You might be looking at a mountain, and you have relaxed into the effortlessness of your present awareness, and then suddenly the mountain is all, you are nothing. Your separate-self sense is suddenly and totally gone, and there is simply everything that is arising moment to moment. You are perfectly aware, perfectly conscious, everything seems completely normal, except you are nowhere to be found. You are not on this side of your face looking at the mountain out there; you simply are the mountain, you are the sky, you are the clouds, you are everything that is arising moment to moment, very simply, very clearly, just so. . . .

Moreover, once you glimpse that state—what the Buddhists call One Taste (because you and the entire universe are one taste or one experience)—it becomes obvious that you are not entering this state, but rather, it is a state that, in some profound and mysterious way, has been your primordial condition from time immemorial. You have, in fact, never left this state for a second.

This is why Zen calls it the Gateless Gate: on this side of that realization, it looks like you have to do something to enter that state—it looks like you need to pass through a gate. But when you do so, and you turn around and look back, there is no gate whatsoever, and never has been.

KEN WILBER

Natural
Nirvana

Since all the aspects of one's path to enlightenment—one's innate capacity to attain enlightenment through the path, the path itself, and the results of the path to enlightenment—are devoid of intrinsic existence, they all possess natural nirvana. Through cultivating insight into this natural nirvana, one will be able to dispel and overcome the sufferings resulting from the erroneous understanding of things and events, which is to say, resulting from fundamental ignorance. Not only can the sufferings be removed, but even the propensity for self-grasping ignorance and the imprints left by past ignorant actions can be removed. Thus, one can completely eliminate ignorance in the present, the imprints of it from the past, and the propensity toward ignorance in the future. Transcending all ignorance . . . one naturally becomes free of fear, and one abides in the final and non-abiding nirvana of a buddha.

HIS HOLINESS THE 14TH DALAI LAMA

How to Arrive

Shall I say it again? In order to arrive there,
To arrive where you are, to get from where you
are not,
> You must go by a way wherein there is no ecstasy.
In order to arrive at what you do not know
> You must go by a way which is the way of ignorance.
In order to possess what you do not possess
> You must go by the way of dispossession.
In order to arrive at what you are not
> You must go through the way in which you are not.
And what you do not know is the only thing you know
And what you own is what you do not own
And where you are is where you are not.

T. S. ELIOT (FROM "EAST COKER")

Presence

"Where shall I look for Enlightenment?"

"Here."

"When will it happen?"

"It is happening right now."

"Then why don't I experience it?"

"Because you do not look."

"What should I look for?"

"Nothing. Just look."

"At what?"

"Anything your eyes alight upon."

"Must I look in a special kind of way?"

"No. The ordinary way will do."

"But don't I always look the ordinary way?"

"No."

"Why ever not?"

"Because to look you must be here. You're mostly somewhere else."

ANTHONY DE MELLO

Gently notice when your mind drifts into the elsewhere and elsewhen. When you are not here and now, you are likely lost in a realm of imagination and worry. Simply and gently notice this.

At this moment if you set the alarm to get up at 3:47 this morning and when the alarm rings and you get up and turn it off and say: What time is it? You'd say:
Now. Now.
Where am I?
Here! Here!

Then go back to sleep.
Get up at 9:00 tomorrow. Where am I?
Here!
What time is it?
Now!

Try 4:32 three weeks from next Thurs.
By God
It is—there's no getting away from it—
That's the way it is
That's the
Eternal present

You finally figure out that it's only the clock that's going around . . .
It's doing its thing but you—you're sitting
Here
Right Now
Always

RAM DASS

One Whole Listening

What a beautiful, quiet morning it is! The faint hum of insects, a cool breeze touching the skin. The breathing—do we feel it? The body pulsating with heart beats. People sitting quietly together—are we here?

Is it essentially one whole listening, or are we locked into our private worlds of thinking, remembering, anticipating? Is there, for moments at a time, an open listening that does not create divisions among us? Can this humming, breathing, pulsating presence take the place of fantasizing, worrying, and wanting? . . .

But there is another, utterly simple way of being here. Just talking or reading about it isn't the same as entering deeply into it. Right now can there be simple listening, awaring, being present to what appears as sound and feeling and thinking in the midst of open silence? A vast listening space of no preferences and no judgments—no one here to *do* the listening. It's happening on its own.

Attending to what is taking place from moment to moment isn't a technique—it is what is and that is all!

TONI PACKER

Stop reading now. Spend the next few minutes listening, as if you are hearing sounds for the very first time.

Stand still. The trees ahead and bushes beside you
Are not lost. Wherever you are is called Here,
And you must treat it as a powerful stranger,
Must ask permission to know it and be known.
The forest breathes. Listen. It answers,
I have made this place around you.
If you leave it, you may come back again, saying Here.
No two trees are the same to Raven
No two branches are the same to Wren.
If what a tree or a bush does is lost on you,
You are surely lost. Stand still. The forest knows
Where you are. You must let it find you.

DAVID WAGONER

You are always Here. Where else could you be?
What a relief.

Peter: Do you think I could say something right now that would displace all your self-doubt and uncertainty?

Rob: Possibly. I've read many stories about teachers who have awakened their students just through saying one or two words.

Peter: What would you say is happening now?

Rob: I'm just saying that historically many people have been awakened through the skill of their teachers. Sometimes their teachers didn't even have to say anything. They just looked at them in a particular way, or drew their attention to the moon in the sky, or something like that.

Peter: What are you doing?

[Silence] *Rob:* I see. I'm beginning to build up a story that if I hang out with teachers for long enough they might zap me. I'm creating another key.

[Long silence] *Peter:* I just want to clarify that I'm not rejecting that there are people, books, teachings, practices and so on, that can help open up a more spacious way of being. Clearly, there are. I'm also not rejecting that teachers can, on occasions, open people up through very minimalist interventions if a person is poised for such a breakthrough. This does happen. But it is also very easy for us to be sidetracked through some fantasy that there is a technique, book, insight or glance that will "do the trick" once and forever.

PETER FENNER

Are you waiting for a master to zap you into permanent bliss-peace? How do you live your life when you are waiting for this imagined event?

Carefree Presence

One cannot seek happiness, for it is the result of realizing the Truth. The personality, which has security and pleasure as its aims, cannot be happy. Pursuing pleasure or safety will entail covering up any unpleasant or frightening truths. This automatically closes Joy. For Joy is the radiance of the heart when Truth is appreciated.

The state of Joy is that of lightness, delight, enjoyment, happiness and sweetness. One becomes a radiance, a playfulness, a carefree presence. One delights in reality. One sees life as a light and playful adventure. Every moment is a source of singular joy, for it is the very presence of Truth. One realizes that Joy is the radiance of Love, which is the breath of Truth.

H. ALMAAS

Your True Nature Now

I n Seattle someone asked Ajahn Chah to describe how he prepared his mind for meditation, and he said, "I just keep it where it always is."

AJAHN CHAH

Meditation is your true nature now.

RAMANA MAHARSHI

"Now!" Balanchine used to say to his dancers. "What are you saving it for? Do it now!" As a boy in St. Petersburg, Balanchine lived through the Russian Revolution and civil war, and the privations of that period left a permanent mark on him. By the time he graduated from school, he was spitting blood. Later, after he escaped to Europe, in 1924, he was diagnosed with tuberculosis, and spent three months in a sanatorium. For years afterwards, he was assailed by afternoon fevers and sweats. "You know, I am really a dead man," he said to one of his early dancers. "I was supposed to die and I didn't, so now everything I do is second chance . . . I don't look back, I don't look forward. Only now."

JOAN ACOCELLA

On the surface it seems that the present moment is only one of many, many moments. Each day of your life appears to consist of thousands or moments where different things happen. Yet if you look more deeply, is there not only one moment, ever? Is life not ever not "this moment"?

ECKHART TOLLE

Wildflower Saints

There are so many [leaves]. Piles of them. I take pleasure in their abundance. More saints than you could ever dream of. Each one singular. Each one itself. Yellow, red, orange, parchment. They sail down in the autumn air like fearless sky divers. They are so trusting—letting go, completely. Not questioning as I do . . . Will it be safe? Will I understand? Will it hurt? . . . stalling, qualifying, questioning, instead of releasing and taking to the air . . .

The wildflower saints provoke me to remember the steadiness of return, year after year. They tell me that one does not need to be cultivated to be beautiful.

GUNILLA NORRIS

You do not need to cultivate your self, mind, or nature. You are beautiful right now.

Seeing
Notions

When I say that this present moment includes all past, present, and future, it's important to remember that this present moment itself does not exist, it too is just another notion. Every idea we have binds and restricts us. When we let go of all our ideas, we see there are no inherent limitations. That's what is so wonderful! We say that we are limited in such and such ways—for example, we can't fly. But these are notions, nothing more. If I can see life as One Body, that this is all one thing, then of course I can fly. I can do anything because I am everything. And I am doing it all right now! I am flying. I am circling the earth, circling Mars, creating stars. If I say I can't fly, all that really means is that my concept of "I" can't fly. Because my idea of me is this limited, bound self, I don't see that I am one with the eagle. As a boundless, unlimited being, I can certainly fly. . . .

The point is that our notion of the present moment is not the moment as it is, it's just a notion. At the same time, this notion is quite useful. In general, we can say this: Seeing notions for what they are, use them as devices; don't be used by them. We're used by them when we cling or are attached to them.

BERNIE GLASSMAN

We have lived our lives so superficially and then suffered for that superficiality, because within each one of us there is this depth of truth, this depth of being that wants Itself known, wants Itself felt, expressed, met. As long as there is a settling for the thought, "Well, I feel this is the truth, therefore it is the truth," then the deeper revelation is overlooked, is missed. Tragically missed. The invitation from Papaji, when he says "to stop," is really to stop telling your story. For one instant. Less than an instant. Stop telling your story. Even if it is a good story, just stop, and immediately the truth is told. You cannot tell your story if you are telling the truth. And you cannot tell the truth if you are telling your story. It is so obvious, isn't it?"

GANGAJI

The Situation of Nowness

Once you begin to deal with a person's whole case history, trying to make it relevant to the present, the person begins to feel that he has no escape, that his situation is hopeless, because he cannot undo his past. He feels trapped by his past with no way out. This kind of treatment is extremely unskilled. It is destructive because it hinders involvement with the creative aspect of what is happening now, what is here, right now . . .

We must simplify rather than complicate the problem with theories of any kind. The situation of nowness, this very moment, contains whole case histories and future determinations. Everything is right here, so we do not have to go any further than this to prove who we were or are or might be. As soon as we try to unravel the past, then we are involved with ambition and struggle in the present, not being able to accept the present moment as it is. It is very cowardly.

CHÖGYAM TRUNGPA

Be brave. Everything relevant is here now.

No Practice

Here and now you know your faults
Drop them and be done with it
What is there to seek?
Child from the south with top knot
Journeys in vain through one hundred castles
Wandering toward the hazy waters

JAKUSHITSU

In an old Buddhist text, the child from the South visited fifty-three different teachers in his search for enlightenment. How many teachers will you consult? How many methods will you try? Until you stop and see.

Stop Reading for a Moment

Stop reading for a moment, and imagine that you are going to die in one minute. The last things you are going to experience are reading these pages, sitting in this room, wearing the clothes you are wearing, thinking and feeling what you are thinking and feeling right now. This is it. This is the end of your life. You have no time to do anything about it. You have no time to write a note or make a phone call. Your life is over. You will die in one minute. All you can do is experience what is, right now.

This is a very simple exercise, but it is quite profound. It brings you into presence very quickly. The projections of the six realms[9] subside. You stop fighting, you stop needing, you stop being concerned with physical comfort, you stop wanting, you stop achieving, and you stop maintaining. Enlightenment, attainment, realization all become meaningless. You are just present. This is one way to cut the web of existence. Be absolute about this point.

KEN MCLEOD

---

[9]In Buddhism, there are said to be six realms of existences—heavens, hells, humans, hungry spirits, animals, and fighting gods.

[Larry Shainberg—"Larry-san"—was
a student of Kyudo Roshi, a Japanese
Zen teacher who spoke little English.]

When I tell Kyudo Roshi that I am studying to become a monk, a look of incredulity crosses his face. Then he explodes with laughter. "You monk? Larry-san a monk? Ha! Ha! Ha!"

For a moment, I think he'll never again regain control of himself, but then suddenly his laughter stops and he fixes me with a stare. "No, Larry-san, you not monk. You *instant monk!* Understand? Instant monk! Listen: I monk. Become monk six years old. Four years temple, fifteen years monastery. Why you want to monk?"

Stammering slightly, I tell him I want to "take my practice to a deeper level."

"Deeper level?" He laughs again. "What you mean 'deeper'? Zen practice only one level. No deep, understand? No shallow."

LAWRENCE SHAINBERG

Deeper. Higher. Better. Impossible. Nowhere to
go but here. Only this.

135

All
the
Way
Now

If we insist that it takes time, then I'm afraid we're still hiding something. It's just a matter of honesty and willingness. Are you willing to take it all the way? Are you willing to take it all the way *now*?

Life is only now.
Love is only now.
Truth is only now.
Wisdom is only now.

Enlightenment, Self Realization—only now.
Joy is only now.
Happiness is only now.
Freedom, only now.
Absolute Peace, only now.

It's up to you.

SCOTT MORRISON

Q: To integrate and strengthen the mind is not an easy task! How does one begin?

N: You can start only from where you are. You are here and now, you cannot get out of here and now.

Q: But what *can* I do here and now?

N: You can be aware of your being—here and now.

Q: That is all?

N: That is all. There is nothing more to it.

Q: All my waking and dreaming, I am conscious of myself. It does not help me much.

N: You were aware of thinking, feeling, doing. You were not aware of your *being*.

Q: What is the new factor you want me to bring in?

N: The attitude of pure witnessing, of watching the events without taking part in them.

SRI NISARGADATTA MAHARAJ

Look
under
Foot

The lesson which life repeats and constantly enforces is "Look under foot."

You are always nearer to the divine and the true sources of your power

than you think.

The lure of the distant and the difficult is deceptive.

The great opportunity is where you are.

Do not despise your own place and hour.

Every place is under the stars, every place is the center of the world.

JOHN BURROUGHS

Sky-Gazing Meditation

Find a comfortable seat outside, preferably with a view. Close your eyes. Take a few deep breaths and let go. Rest naturally and at ease in your body.

Allow all sense experiences to pass, like clouds in a vast, clear sky. Simply observe. Be still. Everything is right here. Let go and let be. Nothing to do; nothing to figure out, understand or achieve. Simply present. At home and at ease. Allow breathing to move in and out, on its own. Let body and mind settle naturally in its own place, in its own time.

Now, slowly open your eyes and elevate them skyward. Gaze evenly into the infinite sky with quiet eyes. Space like mind has no beginning or end, no inside or outside, no actual form, color, size, or shape. Let go and relax the mind, allowing it to dissolve into this infinite, empty spacious awareness.

Allow thoughts, feelings, and sensations to come and go freely, casting everything off into vast sky-mind. Let go. Let be. At ease. As is. In the vast, empty perfect spaciousness of the sky. This is pristine awareness, the innate Great Perfection.

LAMA SURYA DAS

Truth Is Not Far Away

If you cannot find the truth where you are, Where do you expect to find it?

Truth is not far away; it is ever present. It is not something to be attained since not one of your steps leads away from it.

DOGEN

Meditation is running into reality. It does not insulate you from the pain of life. It allows you to delve so deeply into life and all its aspects that you pierce the pain barrier and go beyond suffering.

HENEPOLA GUNARATANA

Finally it has penetrated my thick skull. This life—this moment—is no dress rehearsal. This is it.

F. KNEBEL

Listen to your life.
All moments are key moments.

FREDERICK BUECHNER

141

In the Garden

We cannot separate ourselves from anything. Some say that the gift we have of intellectual capacity is our greatest liability. Our facility to think with discrimination has as its by-product a feeling of separation—this is what has removed us from the Garden of Eden. If we are able to let go of this separation and alienation, we will become aware that we have been in the Garden all along without realizing it. This is the hidden truth of divine union, the recognition that everything is a part of us, that we do not really exist as we think we are. Every aspect of separation comes from deluded thinking.

DAVID A. COOPER

What a lovely garden, hiding in plain sight. See it?

Do You See the Stars?

Once Patrul Rinpoche [Abu] was living with us disciples on this side of the hermitage. Every day at dusk, Abu would do a meditation session on the training of sky gazing, stretched out on his back on a new woolen on a piece of grass the size of himself. One evening, while he was lying there, he said to me, "Lungchey, did you say that you do not know the essence of the mind?" I answered, "Yes, sir, I don't." Abu said, "Oh, there is nothing not to know. Come here." So I went over to him. He said, "Lie down as I am lying down and look at the sky." As I did so the conversation went as follows:

"Do you see the stars in the sky?" "Yes."

"Do you hear the dogs barking in Dzogchen monastery?" "Yes."

"Well, that is meditation."

At that moment, I arrived at the certainty of realization within myself. I have been liberated from the fetters of "it is" and "it is not." I had realized the primordial wisdom, the naked union of emptiness and intrinsic awareness.

PATRUL RINPOCHE

Do you hear the sounds of the street right now? Do you hear the wind in the trees? This is meditation.

143

Everything
Is
God

There is only one world, the world pressing against you this minute.

STORM JAMESON

Everything in life comes to you as a teacher.
Pay attention.
Learn quickly.

OLD CHEROKEE WOMAN TO HER GRANDSON

I was six when I saw that everything was God, and my hair stood up, and all that," Teddy said. "It was on a Sunday, I remember. My sister was only a very tiny child then, and she was drinking her milk and all of a sudden I saw that *she* was God and the *milk* was God. I mean, all she was doing was pouring God into God, if you know what I mean.

J. D. SALINGER (EXCERPT FROM THE SHORT STORY "TEDDY")

One Vast Hymn

[Neurologist Dr. Oliver Sacks was convalescing from a serious leg injury.]

After breakfast I wandered out—it was a particularly glorious September morning—settled myself on a stone seat with a large view in all directions, and filled and lit my pipe. This was a new, or at least almost-forgotten, experience. *I had never had the leisure to light a pipe before*, or not, it seemed to me, for fourteen years at least. Now, suddenly, I had an immense sense of leisure, an unhurriedness, a freedom I had almost forgotten—but which, now it had returned, seemed the most precious thing in life. There was an intense sense of stillness, peacefulness, joy, a pure delight in the "now," freed from drive or desire. I was intensely conscious of each leaf, autumn-tinted, on the ground; intensely conscious of the Eden around me. . . . The world was motionless, frozen—everything concentrated in an intensity of sheer being . . .

Now, on this morning, as though on the first morning of Creation, I felt like Adam beholding a new world with wonder. I had not known, or had forgotten, that there could be such beauty, such completeness, in every moment. I had no sense at all of moments, of the serial, only of the perfection and beauty of the timeless now . . .

OLIVER SACKS

145

The Whole Point

The whole point of life is to live NOW in this present moment, always. If one makes a fetish of improving conditions in the future, one lives neither in the apparent present nor in the illusory future.

The present moment is the eternal moment. There is no eternity but NOW, before time ever was.

RAMESH S. BALSEKAR

Fill in the blank: "I will be happy when _____"
Really?

To
See
Clearly

In good time we shall see
God and his light, you say.
Fool, you shall never see
What you do not see today!

ANGELUS SILESIUS

To see clearly is poetry, philosophy, and religion, all in one.

JOHN RUSKIN

Are you searching for new territory and missing
what is in front of your nose right now?

Direct
Relationship

If one is really serious about all this, one can only begin with what is. The what is in this case is our self, just as we are, at any given moment. We are the content of our consciousness, which must be understood *now*. This demands self-recollectedness, or awareness, in the present moment only. We must be in direct relationship with whatever the wheel of life has brought to our attention. . . .

Each moment is extremely important when one realizes how only in the ever present now, is the door to freedom open.

ALBERT BLACKBURN

It's not about how long you've forgotten, but about remembering now. Start now. No such thing as "too late."

When you put your mind to such a simple, innocent thing, for example, as making a water color, you lose some of the anguish which derives from being a member of a world gone mad. Whether you paint flowers, stars, horses or angels you acquire respect and admiration for all the elements which go to make up our universe. You don't call flowers friends, and stars enemies, or horses Communists, and angels Fascists. You accept them for what they are and you praise God that they are what they are. You desist from improving the world or even yourself. You learn to see not what you want to see but what is. And what is is usually a thousand times better than what might be or ought to be.

If we could stop tampering with the universe we might find it a far better world than we think it to be. After all, we've only occupied it a few hundred million years, which is to say that we are just beginning to get acquainted with it. And if we continue another billion years there is nothing to assure us that we will eventually know it. In the beginning as in the end, it remains a mystery. And the mystery exists or thrives in every smallest part of the universe. It has nothing to do with size or distance, with grandeur or remoteness. Everything hinges upon how you look at things.

HENRY MILLER

Is reality broken? Are you trying to fix it?

Seeing the Secret

When I was on the Squarehead square rigger, bound for Buenos Aires. Full moon in the Trades. The old hooker driving fourteen knots. I lay on the bowsprit, facing astern, with the water foaming into spume under me, the masts with every sail white in the moonlight, towering high above me. I became drunk with the beauty and singing rhythm of it, and for a moment I lost myself—actually lost my life. I was set free! I dissolved in the sea, became white sails and flying spray, became beauty and rhythm, became moonlight and the ship and the high dim-starred sky! I belonged, without past or future, within peace and unity and a wild joy, within something greater than my own life, or the life of Man, to Life itself! To God, if you want to put it that way. . . .

And several other times in my life, when I was swimming far out, or lying alone on a beach, I have had the same experience. Became the sun, the hot sand, green seaweed anchored to a rock, swaying in the tide. Like a saint's vision of beatitude. Like the veil of things as they seem drawn back by an unseen hand. For a second you see—and seeing the secret, are the secret.

EUGENE O'NEILL (FROM *LONG DAY'S JOURNEY INTO NIGHT*)

To be great, be whole; exclude
Nothing, exaggerate nothing that is you.
Be whole in everything. Put all you are
Into the smallest thing you do.
The whole moon gleams in every pool,
It rides so high.

FERNANDO PESSOA

Radical
Acceptance

The way out of our cage begins with *accepting absolutely everything* about ourselves and our lives, by embracing with wakefulness and care our moment-to-moment experience. By accepting absolutely everything, what I mean is that we are aware of what is happening within our body and mind in any given moment, without trying to control or judge or pull away. I do not mean that we are putting up with harmful behavior—our own or another's. *This is an inner process of accepting our actual present-moment experience.* It means feeling sorrow or pain without resisting. It means feeling desire or dislike for someone or something without judging ourselves for the feeling of being driven to act on it.

Clearly recognizing what is happening inside us, and regarding what we see with an open, kind and loving heart, is what I call Radical Acceptance. If we are holding back from any part of our experience, if our heart shuts out any part of who we are and what we feel, we are fueling the fears and feelings of separation that sustain the trance of unworthiness. Radical Acceptance directly dismantles the very foundations of this trance.

TARA BRACH, PHD

Sit quietly for a few moments. Thoughts will naturally arise in your mind. This is all right: The mind was made to make and contain thoughts.

However, as each thought comes up from the depths of your mind, simply say, "Who?"

At first, you will wait for an answer.

Eventually an answer will come, when the discursive mind—the mind of the ego, which constantly discusses the world with itself—quiets down enough to hear the sound of the Still Small Voice. The answer will be the One who is questioning. It is God seeking God.

JASON SHULMAN

Everything's Good

Everything's good . . . Everything. Man is unhappy because he doesn't know he's happy. It's only that. That's all, that's all! If anyone finds out, he'll become happy at once, that minute.

FYODOR DOSTOYEVSKY

Dear Leonard, to look life in the face, always to look life in the face, and to know what it is, to love it for what it is. At last to know it. To love it for what it is. And then to put it away.

VIRGINIA WOOLF IN *THE HOURS* (DAVID HARE, SCREENWRITER)

The ego-climber is like an instrument that's out of adjustment. He's here but he's not here. He rejects the here, is unhappy with it, wants to be further up the trail but when he gets there will be just as unhappy because then it will be "here." What he is looking for, what he wants, is all around him, but he doesn't see that it is all around him. Every step's an effort both physically and spiritually because he imagines his goal to be external and distant.

ROBERT PIRSIG

Every step in the process of taking pictures is a step toward the light, an experience of the holy, an encounter with the God who is at eye level, whose image I see wherever I look.

Making a portrait of someone is an honor and a privilege. It is an opportunity to look deeply into another, to see the essence of spirit as it sweeps across the surface. To do this the photographer must cross a certain threshold, enter into the presence of another being with full attention. The encounter is a holy moment, a time of communion, a chance to reflect and reveal another dimension of the Divine.

JAN PHILLIPS

To look, really look at another, is to see ourselves for the first time.

What If?

Most of us go through each day looking for what we saw yesterday. And, not surprisingly, that is what we find. Most of us expect the same, or worse, and we are not frequently disappointed. But what would happen if we started to expect surprise? What if we removed the blinders that allow us to see only more of the negative things we have come to expect in life? What if we started to look for the ordinary magic? Would we be disappointed?

What would happen to us if we really fell in love with life? How would our lives change if we really thought, as Thoreau encourages, that reality is *fabulous*? What if we took his advice and "steadily observed reality only"? Would our lives really be like a fairy tale, as he suggests? What if we started to look for the grand things that life would bring us each day? Would we be fools of whom other people take advantage, or would we find that life is exciting, joyful, and wonderful?

JAMES A. KITCHENS

Spiritual liberation is not somewhere in the sky. It is found right here in the everyday and ordinary.

The Little Duck

Now we are ready to look
at something pretty special.
It is a duck riding the ocean
a hundred feet beyond the surf,
as he cuddles in the swells.
There is a big heaving in the Atlantic,
and he is part of it.
He can rest while the Atlantic heaves,
because he rests in the Atlantic.
Probably he doesn't *know*
how large the ocean is.
And neither do you.
But he *realizes* it.
And what does he do, I ask you?
He sits down in it.
He reposes in the immediate
as if it were infinity—which it is.
That is religion, and the duck has it.
How about you?

DONALD C. BABCOCK

God
Is

God is in the water of the lake; he is
also in the cracked bed of the lake
when the lake has dried up.

God is in the abundant harvest; he is
also in the famine that occurs when
the harvest fails.

God is in the lightning; he is also in
the darkness when the lightning has
faded.

MANSUR AL-HALLAJ

In every situation and interaction today, remind
yourself, "This is it!"

Look
without
Condemnation

Look lovingly upon the present,
for it holds the only things that are forever true.
All healing lies within it.

When you have learned to look on everyone
with no reference at all to the past,
either his or yours as you perceive it,
you will be able to learn from what you see *now*.

To be born again is to let the past go,
and look without condemnation upon the present.

The present is before time was,
and will be when time is no more.
In it are all things that are eternal,
and they are one.

Fear is not of the present,
but only of the past and future,
which do not exist.
Why wait for Heaven?
It is here today.

A COURSE IN MIRACLES

In
Season

Above all, we cannot afford not to live in the present. He is blessed over all mortals who loses no moment of the passing life in remembering the past. Unless our philosophy hears the cock crow in every barnyard within our horizon, it is belated. That sound commonly reminds us that we are growing rusty and antique in our employments and habits of thought. His philosophy comes down to a more recent time than ours. There is something suggested by it that is a newer testament—the gospel according to this moment. He has not fallen astern; he has got up early and kept up early, and to be where he is is to be in season, in the foremost rank of time. It is an expression of the health and soundness of Nature, a brag for all the world—healthiness as of a spring burst forth, a new fountain of the Muses, to celebrate this last instant of time . . .

HENRY DAVID THOREAU

If people seek Buddha outside of birth and death, that is like heading north to go south, like facing south to try to see the North Star; accumulating causes of birth and death all the more, they have lost the way to liberation. Simply understanding that birth and death is itself nirvana, there is nothing to reject as birth and death, nothing to seek as nirvana. Only then will one have some measure of detachment from birth and death. . . .

There is a very easy way to become a Buddha: not doing any evil, having no attachment to birth and death, sympathizing deeply with all beings, respecting those above, sympathizing with those below, not feeling aversion or longing for anything, not thinking or worrying—this is called Buddha. Don't seek it anywhere else.

DOGEN

Everything
Is
Worship

Surrendering all thoughts of outcome,
unperturbed, self-reliant,
[the sage] does nothing at all, even
when fully engaged in actions.

There is nothing that he expects,
nothing that he fears. Serene,
free from possessions, untainted,
acting with the body alone,

content with whatever happens,
unattached to pleasure or pain,
success or failure, he acts
and is never bound by his actions.

When a man has let go of attachments,
when his mind is rooted in wisdom,
everything he does is worship
and his actions all melt away.

BHAGAVAD GITA

Create a Little Shift

So the crux of zazen [Zen meditation] is this: all we must do is constantly to create a little shift from the spinning world we've got in our heads to right-here-now. That's our practice. The intensity and ability to be right-here-now is what we have to develop. We have to be able to develop the ability to say, "No, I won't spin off up here" to make that choice. Moment by moment our practice is like a choice, a fork in the road: we can go this way, we can go that way. It's always a choice, moment by moment, between our nice world that we want to set up in our heads and what really is. And what really is, at a Zen sesshin,[10] is often fatigue, boredom, and pain in our legs. What we learn from having to sit quietly with that discomfort is so valuable that if it didn't exist, it should. When you're in pain, you can't spin off. You have to stay with it. There's no place to go. So pain is really valuable.

CHARLOTTE JOKO BECK

When we begin to welcome thoughts, spinning off actually becomes a golden opportunity, allowing us to uncover and undo many unquestioned assumptions and stories.

---

[10] *Sesshin*—a week-long Zen meditation retreat.

Dropping
Down

We are just sitting here and, in only one second, you're in being. When I say you're in being, there's no "you" that's in it—it's just the sense of being at home. And it's not something that you did because being was always here. It's just that instead of attention being paid to the activity of mentation, it drops down. And it's not a voluntary thing that anybody is doing—it's being. So there's nobody that can do it. But to say in an absolute kind of way that nobody can do it is misleading. The doer you think you are cannot do it, which is more clear than to say you can't do it. Do you understand what I am saying?

ISAAC SHAPIRO

Your mind makes everything. If you think something is difficult, it is difficult. If you think something is easy, it is easy. If you think that something is not easy, but also not difficult, then it's not difficult or easy. Then what is it really like? Go drink some water, and then you will understand on your own, whether it is hot or cold. Don't make difficult or easy. Don't make anything: when you are doing something, just *do* it. That is Zen.

We all have questions about this life. This is why we practice. "What is Buddha?" "What is mind?" "What is consciousness?" "What is life and death?" If you want to understand the realm of Buddha, first you must keep a mind that is clear like space. That is already every Buddha's mind. Keeping your mind clear like space means your mind is clear like a mirror: when red comes before the mirror, red appears; white comes, white. The name we sometimes give to this is reflect mind. You just reflect the universe exactly as it is. That is already truth.

SEUNG SAHN

What would your life be like without the concepts of "difficult" or "easy"?

Effort and What Is

Effort is a distraction from "what is." The moment I accept "what is" there is no struggle. Any form of struggle or strife is an indication of distraction, and distraction which is effort must exist as long as psychologically I wish to transform "what is" into something it is not. Take, for example, anger. Can anger be overcome by effort, by various methods and techniques, by meditation and various forms of transforming "what is" into "what is not"? Now, suppose that instead of making an effort to transform anger into non-anger, you accepted or acknowledged that you are angry, what would happen then? You would be aware that you are angry. What would happen? Would you indulge in anger? If you are aware that you are angry, which is "what is," and knowing the stupidity of transforming "what is" into "what is not," would you still be angry? If instead of trying to overcome anger, modifying or changing it, you accepted it and looked at it, if you were completely aware of it, without condemning or justifying it, there would be an instantaneous change . . .

So, effort is non-awareness . . . So, awareness is non-effort.

J. KRISHNAMURTI

Throughout my life, I tried to fix people and situations. Assuming a God-like role, I sought to remake the world in my image. How uncomfortable. How pointless.

Be Intimate

Once I was sitting in on an interview at the Cambridge Zen Center and a man came in who was extremely excited, saying he'd just had an enlightenment experience. He described it in great detail. The teacher listened, and in the kindest possible way asked, "Can you show me this experience right now?" He was letting the student know that if the experience happened in the past, he didn't really have it anymore. What is important is what is happening now.

We often have the feeling, about one thing or another in our lives: If only this weren't here I would be happy. If only I weren't afraid, or angry or lonely. If only I didn't have to do the dishes, or take out the trash, or do my income tax. If only I weren't old, if I weren't sick, if I didn't have to die. But those things are here. This is the situation as it is. And none of it keeps you from practicing. None of it really keeps you from being happy. It is what you do with it that makes a difference.

And the thing to do is always the same: Give yourself to it completely. Be intimate.

LARRY ROSENBERG

Take
Off
Your
Shoes

For my own part I am pleased enough with surfaces—in fact they alone seem to me to be of much importance. Such things for example as the grasp of a child's hand in your own, the flavor of an apple, the embrace of friend or lover, the silk of a girl's thigh, the sunlight on rock and leaves, the feel of music, the bark of a tree, the abrasion of granite and sand, the plunge of clear water into a pool, the face of the wind—what else is there? What else do we need?

EDWARD ABBEY

Taking off your shoes is a sacred ritual. It is a hallowed moment of remembering the goodness of space and time. It is a way of celebrating the *holy ground* on which you stand. If you want to be a child of wonder, cherish the truth that time and space are holy. Whether you take your shoes off symbolically or literally matters little. What is important is that you are alive to the *holy ground* on which you stand and to the *holy ground* that you are.

MACRINA WIEDERKEHR

Feel the holy ground now.

The Moment Was All Right

[During a meditation retreat in France, writer Natalie Goldberg suffered a serious dog bite.]

I looked away as the doctor worked. A second felt like a year. He hummed a little. We were alone in the room. Okay, Nat, what are you going to do now? Breathing in and knowing it wasn't quite enough. I was facing the wall. I began to sing a song I'd learned at the retreat. I sang it loud. The lines, "I'm as solid as a mountain, as firm as the earth," comforted me the most. I repeated them over and over and skipped the rest of the song. Here I was, lying out on the table in a French hospital, my leg torn, my pants bloody, the only English I'd heard was "okay." I was alone, and at the other end of my leg, a doctor was performing unspeakable acts while I looked at the wall—and I was singing. Was this possible? I was filled with joy. I felt such gratitude to be alive. The air shimmered. I wanted to turn to the doctor and touch him, thank him.

This all happened in the moment, instantaneously. There was no lag time. I didn't realize a week later that I was okay or that everything was all right. The moment was all right when it was the moment, not later.

NATALIE GOLDBERG

Immensity Awaits You

Q: I have brief glimpses of this realm in moments of stillness. Then I go to work and find myself in an environment, which is neither royal nor peaceful, and my serenity immediately disappears. How can I keep my equanimity permanently?

A: Everything that appears in awareness is nothing other than awareness: co-workers; clients; superiors; absolutely everything, including the premises, the furniture and the equipment. First understand this intellectually, then verify that this is so. There comes a moment where this feeling of intimacy, this benevolent space around you no longer goes away; you find yourself at home everywhere, even in the packed waiting room of a train station. You only leave it when you go into the past or future. Don't stay in that hovel. This immensity awaits you right here, at this very moment. Being already acquainted with its presence, and once having tasted the harmony underlying appearances, let the perceptions of the external world and your body sensations unfold freely in your welcoming awareness, until the moment that the background of plenitude reveals itself spontaneously.

FRANCIS LUCILLE

Peace has nothing to do with where you are and everything to do with how you see where you are.

When it's time to use the toilet, *really* time, all importance is reduced to the event.

In bed at *that* moment, orgasm is all.

Chased by a madman with a gun, there is *nothing* else; waking up from the dream, there is nothing else but *relief.*

A child finds her doll important. A father finds his finances important.

Riddled with cancer, an old man finds love important, as his eyes close one last time.

What do you find important, now, today? What did you find important ten years ago?

Remember back to your earliest childhood memory, the very first time you can remember anything at all. What was important to you then?

Still feeling your very first memory in life, feel *before* that. What happens when you try to feel earlier than your first memory? Do you feel into blackness? Is there a sharp wall of time that stops you? Or can you feel an ineffable openness that seems to extend before your earliest childhood memory, an openness without clear bounds, an openness that is you even now?

Of every moment that has ever seemed important, all that remains is the openness who you are.

DAVID DEIDA

Be Absolutely Still

Q: What do I have to do to wake up to my true Self?

A: You have to do nothing to wake up. Nothing! Isn't this the last thing you expected? This is the last place you thought to look. Everyone is scurrying to do something to get awakeness. Everyone is reading, retreating, and practicing just to wake up. If it is as complicated as doing something then this implies that you are separate from that which is awake. You are not separate from what is awake. You are That. Don't do anything. Don't even not do anything. Be absolutely still.

GANGAJI

Effortlessly Witness

So let's start by just being aware of the world around us. Look out there at the sky, and just relax your mind, let your mind and the sky mingle. Notice the clouds floating by in the sky. Notice that this takes no effort on your part. Your present awareness, in which these clouds are floating, is very simple, very easy, effortless, spontaneous. You simply notice that there is an *effortless awareness* of the clouds. The same is true of those trees, and those birds, and those rocks. You simply and effortlessly witness them.

Look at the thoughts arising in your own mind. You might notice various images, symbols, concepts, desires, hopes and fears, all *spontaneously* arising in your awareness. They arise, stay a bit, and pass. These thoughts and feelings arise in your present awareness, and that awareness is very simple, effortless, spontaneous. You simply and effortlessly witness them.

So notice: you can see the clouds float by, because you are *not* those clouds—you are the witness of those clouds. You can feel bodily feelings, because you are *not* those feelings—you are the witness of those feelings. You can see thoughts float by, because you are *not* those thoughts, you are the witness of those thoughts. Spontaneously and naturally, these things all arise, on their own, in your present, *effortless* awareness.

KEN WILBER

This
Eye
of
Mine

All this universe is in this eye of mine.

SEPPO

To the one who knows how to look and feel, every moment of this free wandering life is an enchantment.

ALEXANDRA DAVID-NEEL

All waiting is futile. To depend on time to solve our problems is self-delusion. The future, left to itself, merely repeats the past. Change can only happen now, never in the future.

SRI NISARGADATTA MAHARAJ

It is eternity now. I am in the midst of it. It is about me in the sunshine; I am in it, as the butterfly in the light-laden aire. Nothing has to come; it is now. Now is eternity.

RICHARD JEFFERIES

I once saw a simple fish pond in a Japanese village which was perhaps eternal. A farmer made it for his farm. The pond was a simple rectangle, about 6 feet wide, and 8 feet long; opening off a little irrigation stream . . . In the pond there were eight great ancient carp, each maybe 18 inches long, orange, gold, purple, and black: the oldest one had been there eighty years. The eight fish swam, slowly, slowly, in circles—often within the wooden circle. The whole world was in that pond. Every day the farmer sat by it for a few minutes. I was there only one day and I sat by it all afternoon. Even now, I cannot think of it without tears. Those ancient fish had been swimming, slowly, in that pond for eighty years. It was so true to the nature of the fish, and flowers, and the water, and the farmers, that it had sustained itself for all that time, endlessly repeating, always different. There is no degree of wholeness or reality which can be reached beyond that simple pond.

And yet, like the other words, this word [eternal] confuses more than it explains. It hints of a religious quality. The hint is accurate. And yet it makes it seem as though the quality which that pond has is a mysterious one. It is not mysterious. It is above all ordinary. What makes it eternal is its ordinariness. The word "eternal" cannot capture that.

CHRISTOPHER ALEXANDER

Your ordinary life is the great mystery. There is no need to make it artificially holy, mysterious or "other."

Be
Attentive

Do not pay attention or investigate; leave mind in its own sphere . . .

Do not see any fault anywhere,

Do not take anything to heart,

Do not hanker after the signs of progress . . .

Although this may be said to be what is meant by non-attention,

Yet do not fall a prey to laziness;

Be attentive by constantly using inspection.

GAMPOPA

This classic instruction on non-effort still urges us to be attentive. What to do? What not to do? Just simply notice in every moment.

Entrances to holiness are everywhere.
The possibility of ascent is all the time.
Even at unlikely times and through unlikely places.
There is no place on earth without the Presence.

BAMIDBAR RABBA 12:4

Knock! Knock! Who's there?

Precise Awareness

One aim of mindfulness is to keep us attuned to the present. Mindfulness is not thinking *about* what we experience, but a direct, bare attention to the experience itself. Distractedness is one sign that we are avoiding the truth of the moment. A mindful inquiry—What is keeping me from being in the present?—can aid that subtle attunement. Sometimes the answer reveals the hidden influence of our most deeply ingrained emotional patterns . . .

Often the very thing that makes us resist experiencing emotions is our habitual reaction to them. Because of fear or avoidance, we are unable to face the experience as it actually is with a neutral, centered awareness. It's the mental counterpart of shifting our posture to avoid the slightest discomfort.

The power to sustain our awareness with steadiness can cut through the mind's resistance to the reality of the moment. A steady investigation can bring a sense of equanimity to whatever happens. If it is pleasant, be aware without clinging. If it is unpleasant, be aware without resistance. If your response is indifference, precise awareness can prevent it from becoming boring.

TARA BENNETT-GOLEMAN

Perfectly Free

Realize that whatever arises is the display of the absolute,

The primordial nature, unbroken simplicity.

If you don't cling, whatever arises is naturally freed.

Simply remain in the great equal taste, without rejecting or accepting.

Childish sentient beings, not knowing this,

Treat phenomena as if they were solid and real;

Thus begins a chain of attractions and aversions,

And the great sufferings of existence—a nonexistent masquerade!

The powerful roots are

Ignorance and taking beings and phenomena to exist truly;

Conditioned existence comes about

From getting used to those things.

Nothing to illuminate,

Nothing to eliminate,

Looking perfectly at perfection itself,

Seeing perfection, one is perfectly free.

SHECHEN GYALTSAP

The Stop Sign Meditation

The other morning, I caught myself rushing the toaster. After a few moments of peering into its opening, jostling it, and impatiently trying to force my toast to cook faster, I woke up. I laughed, breathed and smiled, and settled into the present moment. My toaster did its job and produced perfect toast in less than three minutes. I decided to create a stop sign practice out of the experience of toasting bread. The practice is simple. Putting bread into the toaster is my reminder, a visual and kinesthetic stop sign. During the three minutes that the bread is browning, I breathe, and calm my mental and physical activity. Waiting for toast is an opportunity for me to experience peace.

Streets and highways in the United States have a symbol for stopping: a red, octagonal sign with white letters that reads "STOP." In driver's education, we learned that when we see such a sign, we are to make a complete stop with our automobile. We are instructed to be in full awareness, look to our right, look to our left, check the pedestrian crosswalk and our rearview mirrors before proceeding. This is a practice of mindfulness, a practice of stopping . . .

TRACY D. SARRIUGARTE AND PEGGY ROSE WARD

You can invent your own mindfulness practice or follow traditional instructions. Begin with deliberate focus and then gently drop into natural awareness.

Beyond Any Concept

From the contemplative point of view, remaining within "the freshness of the present instant" helps us to recognize the mind's empty and luminous nature and the transparency of the world of phenomena. This nature is immutable, not in the sense of being a sort of permanent entity, but because it is the mind's and phenomena's true mode of existence, beyond any concept of coming and going, being or not being, one or many, beginning or end.

MATTHIEU RICARD

Where Does It Exist?

Master Tung-kuo asked Chuang Tzu, "This thing called the Way—where does it exist?"

Chuang Tzu said, "There's no place, it doesn't exist."

"Come," said Master Tung-kuo, "you must be more specific!"

"It is in the ant."

"As low a thing as that?"

"It is in the panic grass."

"But that's lower still!"

"It is in the tiles and shards."

"How can it be so low?"

"It is in the piss and shit!"

Master Tung-kuo made no reply.

CHUANG TZU

182

Everybody Sits

During the 1960s, many unusual people showed up at the [Zen] monastery gate. Among them was a young electrician from Sweden, whose limited command of English was further hindered by a few beers. He was met at the gate by the director, who asked him what he wanted. "I want to study Buddhism!" the Swede bellowed.

"Have you ever sat?" the director asked, using our shorthand expression for "Have you ever done sitting meditation?"

The Swede didn't know how to answer this question. It seemed to be a question in plain English, and he understood the words, but somehow the meaning eluded him. Was this some kind of Buddhist trick? Was the director making fun of him? Of course he had sat. Finally, he decided that if the question was a trick he would not take the bait. He drew himself up to his full height and shouted, "Everyone has sat!"

The Swede entered the retreat center and remained there for several years. He was right, of course. All people have sat. We do it every day. We stand too, and walk, and lie down.

LEWIS RICHMOND

Why make meditation into some holy and separate ritual when you can sit, stand, walk, and lie down in awareness?

Choose
Life

S ome years ago, when I was teaching meditation at a federal women's prison in California, one of the inmates observed, "When you're in prison, it's especially important to try and live in the present moment. It's easy to get lost in the past, which you can't change anyway, or to get lost hoping for the future, which is not yet here. If you do that, it's like you're not really alive." Then she paused and looked at me, her eyes shining, and said, "I choose life."

SHARON SALZBERG

When you identify with your beliefs, what kind of limiting prison are you creating for yourself?

Interrelatedness

[U Kyi Maung, an 80-year-old freedom fighter, spent 11 years as a political prisoner in Burma.]

As for me, don't worry. What I care about the most, and practice off and on throughout the day, is to be aware. That's all. To be awake. See, I have pieces of paper in my pockets that I carry with me: quotes, inspiring reminders. They refocus my mind on the here and now. That is the most important thing to me. To be present. Awake. Aware. My eleven years in prison were severe, but I used the time to my advantage. I never forget what I am seeing now—the pale green line streaking across the pond, or the shadow of the tree across your leg—disappears the moment I turn my face. This is life's simplicity. Just the here and now. Aware that nothing is permanent.

The barbed-wire fence across the back of Aung San Suu Kyi's compound over there—why worry about the presence of such an irritant? It's insignificant. Now if I worry about anything, it's that I might lose this sense of awareness. So I guard it as something precious. Things pass . . . that I have seen. Life is what you make it now. So let us put our energies into life. Into understanding our interrelatedness.

U KYI MAUNG

Home

First, beware of philosophies that put spiritual concerns into a framework of growth or evolution, which I believe are the great modern idols. Both are important phenomena of eternity's time theater, but as paradigms, they're old hat, hangovers from the age of empire-building and the work ethic.

The "I want it now" attitude, so often deplored by spiritual pundits as a twentieth-century sin, is in my view a very healthy sign that we are beginning to be disillusioned with time-entrapment. A truly mystical paradigm has to be post-evolutionary, a paradigm of *lila*, divine play for its own sake, where any purposes along the line of time, great or small, are subordinate to the divine satisfaction that is always present in each eternal instant. Mystical gnosis is knowing the instant-by-instant delight of Infinite Aliveness in all manifestation, irrespective of whether, from the purely human standpoint, the manifestation is creative or destructive, growing or withering, evolving towards some noetic Omega or fading out. . . .

When the word "home" is used to describe eternity, there is an almost irresistible temptation to think of life as a journey of return, whereas mystical awakening for me has been like Dorothy's in *The Wizard of Oz*: the realization that I never really left home and never could. Here too T. S. Eliot has the words for it: "Home is where one starts from."

JOHN WREN-LEWIS

Radiance

Take the moon reflected on the surface of a lake as an example. It is brilliantly apparent, but you cannot trap it. It is vividly present and at the same time utterly intangible. The same is true of the mind. By its very nature, which is the indivisible union of emptiness and luminosity, nothing can obstruct it and it can obstruct nothing.

It is unlike a solid object, such as a rock, with a physical, exclusive presence. In essence, the mind is insubstantial and omnipresent.

The perceptions of samsara and nirvana are simply the play of the mind's natural creativity, the radiance of its emptiness. The essence of this radiance is emptiness, and the expression of emptiness is radiance. They are indivisible.

DILGO KHYENTSE RINPOCHE

Trust It Once and for All

I always tell you that what is inherent in you is presently active and presently functioning, and need not be sought after, need not be put in order, need not be practiced or proven. All that is required is to trust it once and for all. This saves a lot of energy.

Why don't you understand the essence that has always been there? There is not much to Buddhism; it only requires you to see the way clearly. It does not tell you to extinguish random thoughts and suppress body and mind, shutting your eyes and saying "This is It!" The matter is not like that.

You must observe the present state. What is its logic? What is its guiding pattern? Why are you confused? This is the most direct approach.

FOYAN

Striving is an expression of this confusion. Inquire deeply and see.

All Is a Miracle

I like to walk alone on country paths, rice plants and wild grasses on both sides, putting each foot down on the earth in mindfulness, knowing that I walk on the wondrous earth. In such moments, existence is a miraculous and mysterious reality. People usually consider walking on water or in thin air a miracle. But I think the real miracle is not to walk either on water or in thin air, but to walk on earth. Every day we are engaged in a miracle which we don't even recognize: a blue sky, white clouds, green leaves, the black, curious eyes of a child—our own two eyes. All is a miracle.

THICH NHAT HANH

Looking for special signs and miracles, we can easily miss what is unfolding before us. Your eyes read these words—how wonderful. You are breathing—how miraculous.

Hold Yourself Lightly

When you are awake, at each moment, beauty reveals itself. Photographers spend their lives looking for it—a dune lit by the evening sun, a bluebird in a tree, a mountain with its head in the clouds. In each moment, there is something there, something indefinable, a name that cannot be spoken. For those with the right attention, for those who can see, God pours through every moment, every blade of grass, every flash of a human eye. But to see this, you have to hold yourself lightly, because if you are too attached to your fears, your anger, your shame, then all you can see is yourself. The universe jitterbugs past, with all the presence of God manifest, but without purification, while you sit in the corner whining about your life.

JAMES A. CONNOR

The teacher said: "Everything is God." As he heard this, the adept understood: God is the only reality. The Divine moves in all things, unsuffering, intangible; everything in the world, subject or object, is but the veil of its maya. . . .[11]

He felt as if he were a huge and luminous cloud . . . freed from gravity's sway. In total self-absorption, he kept to the middle of the road, when all at once an elephant approached, marching toward him. The driver, seated high on the animal's neck, shouted down at him: "Give way! Give way!" The adept heard and saw the elephant clearly, in spite of his ecstasy, but he did not get out of its way. He said to himself: "Why should I stand aside? I am God, and the elephant is God. Is God to live in fear of Himself?" Fearlessly he walked towards the animal—and at the last moment the elephant seized him, wrapping him up in its trunk, sweeping him aside and depositing him not very gently in the dust of the roadside.

The adept, completely crushed and covered in dust, went to his teacher and told him of the encounter. The guru said: "You are quite right: you are God and the elephant is God—but why did you not listen to the voice of God speaking to you from above, as the elephant driver?"

INDIAN PARABLE[12]

---

[11]*Maya*—illusion.
[12]From *Wisdom of India* by Heinrich Zimmer.

The Source of a Snowflake

[Les Kaye is both a Zen priest and a business-person.]

My dual careers taught me that sitting on a meditation cushion or in an office, wearing robes or wearing a business suit, are fundamentally not very different. Moving back and forth between formal spiritual practice and the usual activities of everyday life became more and more natural. The workplace became for me a place of fluid relationships rather than an arena of tense confrontations.

My passionate concern for discovering the single, permanent "source" of life evaporated long ago. It was just a feeling, an idea that I once had. Pursuing such a search is as useless as looking for the source of a snowflake. To the strictly analytic mind, the conditions that produce a snowflake—temperature, moisture—do not possess the qualities of snowflakeness. Yet despite what our senses and logic tell us, the unique white crystal appears. The "source" of everything, I discovered, is in the constantly changing present moment.

LES KAYE

192

Q: How can I live in the Now?

Katie: You do. You just haven't noticed.
Only in this moment are we in reality. You and everyone can learn to live in the moment, *as* the moment,
to love whatever is in front of you, to love it as you. If you keep
doing The Work[13] [of inquiry], you will see more and more clearly
what you are without a future or a past. The miracle of love
comes to you in the presence of the uninterpreted moment. If
you are mentally somewhere else, you miss real life.

But even the Now is a concept. Even as the thought completes
itself, it's gone, with no proof that it ever existed, other than as
a concept that would lead you to believe it existed, and now that
one is gone too. Reality is always the story of a past. Before you
can grasp it, it's gone. Each of us already has the peaceful mind
that we seek.

BYRON KATIE

When we idealize living in the present moment,
aren't we just creating another concept? Forget
everything you know about the present
moment and find yourself immediately
immersed in it!

---

[13]"The Work" of Byron Katie is a process of self-inquiry using four questions to investigate
thoughts and beliefs.

The Absurdity

Since our own mind is inherently buddha, all we really need to do is to recognize and rest in our true nature. From this point of view, the awakened state is our own perfectly ordinary mind, our everyday experience. Yet, even after it has been shown to us, we seem unable to retain that realization. Our very attempts to do so get in our way, because they miss the point. We start by making efforts to change ourselves, to find something, or to attain some goal, but these very efforts become counterproductive. In the ultimate sense, there is really nothing to do and nothing to change. Yet we start to have doubts and feel we are unable to achieve anything. We despair at getting nowhere, when really there is nowhere to go. This paradox is highlighted with a series of questions[14] designed to shock us into seeing the absurdity of the whole situation.

FRANCESCA FREEMANTLE

[14]See the next selection for the series of questions.

When the powerful method of entering into this itself is pointed out,

Your own self-knowledge in the present moment is just this!

Your own uncontrived self-illumination is just this,

So why say you can't realize the nature of mind?

There's nothing at all to meditate on within it,

So why say nothing happens when you meditate?

Your own direct experience of awareness is just this,

So why say you can't find your own mind?

Uninterrupted awareness and clarity are just this,

So why say you can't recognize your mind?

The one who thinks about the mind is the mind itself,

So why say you can't find it even when you look?

There's nothing at all to be done to it,

So why say nothing happens whatever you do?

It only needs to be left naturally in its own place,

So why say it will not stay still?

It only needs to be left at ease, doing nothing,

So why say you cannot do that?

Clarity, awareness, and emptiness inseparable are spontaneously present,

So why say your practice is not successful?

. . . Knowing in the present moment is just this,

So why say you do not know it?

PADMASAMBHAVA[15]

---

[15]From *Luminous Emptiness* by Francesca Freemantle.

Holy without Holiness

"You understand," said Chaydem, "but the reality of it escapes you. Understanding is nothing. The eyes must be kept open, constantly. To open your eyes you must relax, not strain. Don't be afraid of falling backwards into a bottomless pit. There is nothing to fall into. You're in it and of it, and one day, if you persist, you will be it. I don't say you will have it, *please* notice, because there's nothing to possess. Neither are you to be possessed, remember that! You are to liberate your self. There are no exercises, physical, spiritual, to practice. All such things are like incense—they awaken a feeling of holiness. We must be holy without holiness. We must be whole . . . complete. That's being holy. Any other kind of holiness is false, a snare, and a delusion . . ."

HENRY MILLER

I spent years trying to be a holy, solemn monk. It was so artificial, unnecessary, and, in retrospect, goofy. I was trying to glow in the dark while in truth everything was naturally radiant.

When you do a thing, do it with the whole self. One thing at a time. Now I sit here and I eat. For me nothing exists in the world except this food, this table. I eat with the whole attention. So you must do—in everything.

GEORGE I. GURDJIEFF

We cannot put off living until we are ready. The most salient characteristic of life is its urgency, "here and now" without any possible postponement. Life is fired at us point-blank.

JOSE ORTEGA Y GASSET

Secularism teaches us to be good here and now. I know of nothing better than good. Secularism teaches us to be just here and now. I know of nothing juster than just.

ROBERT INGERSOLL

Intimacy

Intimacy is an experience of non-separation, of being at one with whatever is happening. We tend to think that we are not all right now—we're too fearful, greedy, angry, whatever—but that if we take up some spiritual practice we can improve ourselves. We will be all right at some moment in the future.

We have "in order to" mind; we are always doing *this* in order to get *that*, or in order to *be* that. Yet that very tendency—to strive, be ambitious, be preoccupied with a goal, get ahead of ourselves—takes us out of the present moment, away from how we are now. It can actually prevent intimacy. Then we complain that we don't have it. Our wish for intimacy can prevent us from being intimate.

LARRY ROSENBERG

Later, he remembered certain moments in which the power of *this* moment was already contained, as in a seed. He thought of the hour in that other southern garden (Capri) when the call of a bird did not, so to speak, break off at the edge of his body, but was simultaneously outside and in his innermost being, uniting both into one uninterrupted space in which, mysteriously protected, only one single place of purest, deepest consciousness remained. On that occasion, he had closed his eyes . . . and the Infinite passed into him from all sides, so intimately that he believed he could feel the stars which had in the meantime appeared, gently reposing within his breast.

RAINER MARIA RILKE

Timeless Quantum Cosmology

Some years ago, I heard Dame Janet Baker interviewed on radio. She was asked if she ever listened to her recordings and, if so, what were her favorites. She said she almost never listened to them. For her, every Now was so exciting and new, it was a great mistake to try to repeat one. In her singing she made no attempt at all to recreate earlier performances and do the high points the same way as the night before. Again and again she spoke with the deepest reverence of the Now and how it should be new and happen spontaneously. "The Now is what is real," she said.

I thought it was the perfect artistic expression of how I see time-less quantum cosmology.

JULIAN BARBOUR

For a long time it had seemed to me that life was about to begin—real life. But there was always some obstacle in the way. Something to be got through first, some unfinished business, time still to be served, a debt to be paid. Then life would begin. At last it dawned on me that these obstacles were my life.

FR. ALFRED D'SOUZA

Makom: The Place

You already are where you need to be. You need go nowhere else. Feel it now in the moisture on your tongue. Sense the effortless filling and emptying of your lungs, the involuntary blinking of your eyes. Just an inch or so behind your sternum where your heart beats. That is where the *makom*[16] is. Right here all along and we did not know it because we were fast asleep, here in this very *makom*.

RABBI LAWRENCE KUSHNER

---

[16]*Makom*—Hebrew for holy place, the place of God. Also another name for God.

I Wrote My Lover a Letter without Words

I said,
I am a small woman,
bold enough to want
to hold a planet in my broken heart.

I said,
Here stillness falls
upon the shoulder of stillness,
as one shadow disappears in another.
Everything is here
in the point of this moment of air.

I said,
Under this hand of silence,
this woman comes to life,
like a waterfall undressing itself.

I said,
Reduced to a needle of light,
I am completely myself.
I said,
In each moment,
the story of the universe is repeated:
There was nothing,
        Look what is coming to be.
You always surprise me.

DEENA METZGER

I ask you to abandon at once all the joy you've ever felt in reading the words of the scriptures yourself or when being aroused and instructed by others. Be totally without knowledge and understanding, as before, like a three-year-old child—though the innate consciousness is there, it doesn't operate. Then contemplate what's there before the thought of seeking the direct essentials arises: observe and observe. As you feel you're losing your grip more and more and your heart is more and more uneasy, don't give up and slack off: this is the place to cut off the heads of the thousand sages. Students of the Path often retreat at this point. If your faith is thoroughgoing, just keep contemplating what's before the thought of seeking instruction in the direct essentials arises. Suddenly you will awaken from your dream, and there won't be any mistake about it.

TA HUI

Real Humanness

In the end, when all the strategies to resist life fall away, what else could remain but a human being? It is deeply saddening to me that much of human endeavor, whether called spiritual or scientific, is unconsciously an effort to escape from human life, to try to live in some fantasy world of spiritual salvation or technological security. Rather than some imagined immunity magically granted by contact with the transcendental, the dance of awakening invites us more fully into life and into conscious responsibility. To be an enlightened person is to be a human being. Yet self transformation is rarely seen in this way because most people are using spirituality and their intellects as the means of escaping the pain and struggle of life, as a way of avoiding relationship to real humanness.

There is, with this deepening attention, a sense that the spiritual is not something that happens when there are paranormal phenomena, or happens in a church, or happens in a place of worship, or happens in Machu Picchu or in the pyramids, or happens in any one of the overly glorified pilgrimage sights that seduce the New Ager. In fact, the Sacred is everywhere. The Sacred is everything. And every one is part of a sacred process.

RICHARD MOSS

I have found over and over again that the place that I run away from is actually where I need to be. So, what do you run away from?

In spite of all similarities, every living situation has, like a newborn child, a new face, that has never been before and will never come again. It demands of you a reaction that cannot be prepared beforehand. It demands nothing of what is past. It demands presence, responsibility; it demands you.

MARTIN BUBER

[Martin Buber] was for me, in every sense of the term, the most human person I have met . . . I think he never despaired because he was ready to meet the new moment in whatever form it came with all of his being. And that perhaps is the secret, if there is one, of dialogue which can never become a technique or a philosophy, but only a living presence which is present to the present-ness of the situation and calls the other into presence too.

MAURICE FRIEDMAN

In the Kitchen

I remember this illumination happening to me one noontime as I stood in the kitchen and watched my children eat peanut butter and jelly sandwiches. We were having a most unremarkable time on a nondescript day, in the midst of the most quotidian of routines. I hadn't censed the table, sprinkled the place mats with holy water, or uttered a sanctifying prayer over the Wonder bread. I wasn't feeling particularly "spiritual." But, heeding I don't know what prompting, I stopped abruptly in mid-bustle, or mid-woolgathering, and looked around me as if I were opening my eyes for the first time that day.

The entire room became luminous and so alive with movement that everything seemed suspended—yet pulsating—for an instant, like light waves. Intense joy swelled up inside me, and my immediate response was gratitude—gratitude for everything, every tiny thing in that space. The shelter of the room became a warm embrace; water flowing from the tap seemed a tremendous miracle; as my children became, for a moment, not my property or my charges or my tasks, but eternal beings of infinite singularity and complexity whom I would one day, in an age to come, apprehend in their splendid fullness.

HOLLY BRIDGES ELLIOT

Illumination is always happening. Sometimes you see it, sometimes you don't.

When you are in the present moment, there is no you that is separate and alone, no identification with egocentricity.

Self-hate is designed to make sure that doesn't happen.

Self-hate will pull you out of the experience of the present moment in order to get you to focus on "What's wrong? What did I do?"

It's that self-conscious questioning and analysis that brings you out of the present moment either into the past, "How should I have been instead of how I was?" Or into the future, "What should I do about it?"

It doesn't matter what did or did not happen then.
It only matters what happens NOW.

CHERI HUBER

Great Perfection

Listen again, my heart-friends!

Don't contrive, don't contrive, don't alter your mind,
Adopting manipulation and modification,
Mind will be disturbed,
And this contrived state of mind
Will obscure the heart of the matter.

Mind-itself, free of fabrication, is one's authentic, original countenance.
Gaze nakedly at this intrinsic nature, without alteration,
Preserving the flow of meditation,
Free of adulteration by artifice.

Free of distraction, free of clinging, free of meditation, beyond intellect:
Remain in the state beyond intellect, Great Perfection.[17]
Selfless, unborn, free of extremes, inexpressible:
Remain in the ineffable nature, Great Perfection.

NYOSHUL KHENPO

You don't have to try to be enlightened, spiritual, or a Buddhist. Just be.

---

[17]Great Perfection *(Dzogchen)* is the highest teaching of the Nyingma school of Tibetan Buddhism.

Staying with the Whatness

Several years ago I was faced with an alarming reading on a screening test for prostate cancer. Instead of having a biopsy, I chose to treat myself with a combination of healing meditation, acupuncture, and herbs for six months. Then I took another test to see to what extent the cancer cells remained, if at all. Aware that it would be very unpleasant to have my prostate removed and that I might then be incontinent and impotent, I felt a great deal of fear while waiting for the results. I practiced staying with the body, asking over and over again, "What *is* this?" The combination of fear and self-pity was powerful, as was the desire to escape, but my continuous effort to return to the physical reality of the moment began to undercut the solidity of my fear. The question "What is this?" worked like a laser in focusing on the experience of fear itself. After two days of practice, I realized that none of what I feared was happening now, nor had it ever happened! There was no real pain other than that generated by my thoughts. This realization effectively burst the bubble of my fears. The insight did not come from thinking but from staying with the "whatness" of the moment. It came from being curious about reality.

EZRA BAYDA

Our minds can create anxiety and suffering simply by conjuring up terrifying future scenarios. I've noticed my imagination is much scarier than reality.

It
Is
Happiness

Do you see O my brothers and sisters?
It is not chaos or death—it is form, union, plan—
it is eternal life—it is Happiness.

WALT WHITMAN

At the end of all things, the blessed will say, "We never lived anywhere but in heaven."

C. S. LEWIS

If for a moment we make way with our petty selves, wish no ill on anyone, apprehend no ill, cease to be but as a crystal which reflects a ray—what shall we not reflect! What a universe will appear crystallized and radiant around us.

HENRY DAVID THOREAU

210

Over and over I come into contact with people who are lost in their spiritual searching or lost in their personal pain because they believe that what they have lived until this moment is what they're going to live from now on. They believe that the past they've lived has conditioned their reality to be the same now and forever. And I think that the greatest miracle of our life here on earth—as well as the great mystery—is that when we stop making assumptions and when we stop pretending to be God, we come to understand that we have absolutely no knowledge about what will happen next. And that lack of any kind of knowing is the very thing which allows us—if we let it seep into every pore of our being—to become available for greater and greater spiritual freedom.

RAPHAEL CUSHNIR

Before
My
Eyes

. . . I would be walking along the street when things would suddenly change before my eyes, to become unbelievably beautiful and *real*. Things scientists tell us about light and sound waves, gravity and atoms and so on were clear and understandable. As also passages in the Bible that had hitherto eluded me . . . Colour was breathtakingly beautiful, everything had significance and *everything and everybody was one.* Not only every other human being, but all animals, plants, stones, everything was one in unity, making nonsense of the view that only human beings have souls. There is no such thing as time as we know it. Everything that is, has been, is and always will be . . . And we are *here and now* in eternity.

RERU ACCOUNT[18]

When we are lost in past and future thinking, we are sleepwalking. The more you wake up to the present moment, the more beauty you will see.

[18]RERU—Religious Experience Research Centre.

The greatest support we can have is mindfulness, which means being totally present in each moment. If the mind remains centered, it cannot make up stories about the injustice of the world or one's friends, or about one's desires or sorrows. All these stories could fill many volumes, but when we are mindful such verbalizations stop. Being mindful means being fully absorbed in the moment, leaving no room for anything else. We are filled with the momentary happening, whatever it is—standing or sitting or lying down, feeling pleasure or pain—and we maintain a nonjudgmental awareness, a "just knowing."

AYYA KHEMA

What a Relief!

"When I was young, the future was where all the good stuff was kept, the pretty clothes, the pretty china, the family silver, the grown-up jobs. The future was a land on its own, and we couldn't wait to get there. Not that youth wasn't great, but it came with disadvantages; I remember the feeling I was missing something really good that was going on somewhere else, somewhere I wasn't. I remember feeling life passing me by. I remember impatience. I don't feel that way now. If something interesting is going on somewhere else, good, thank god, I hope nobody calls me. Sometimes it's all I can do to brush my teeth—toothpaste is just too stimulating.

The future was also the place where the bad stuff waited in ambush. . . . Now I know I can only control my tongue, my temper, and my appetite, but that's it. I have no effect on weather, traffic, or luck. I can't make good things happen. I can't influence the future, and I can't fix the past. What a relief."

ABIGAIL THOMAS

The Buddha taught to lay down those things that lack a real abiding essence. If you lay everything down, you will see the truth. If you don't, you won't. That's the way it is.

And when wisdom awakens within you, you will see truth wherever you look. Truth is all you'll see.

AJAHN CHAH

Do you wish to penetrate directly and be free? When I am talking like this, many people are listening. Quickly! Look at the one who is listening to this talk. Who is he who is listening right now?

BASSUI

Not
Waiting

His disciples said to him, "When will the Kingdom come?"

"It will not come by waiting for it.

It will not be a matter of saying 'here it is' or 'there it is!'

Rather, the kingdom of the father is spread out upon the earth, and men do not see it."

JESUS

Can you see it?

The
True
of
All
Things

To wake up to
who we are
what we are here for.

To make all life
more poetical, more sane
more living, loving

To experience
the true of all things
this moment . . .
this moment . . .
this moment.

WILLIAM SEGAL

The
Only
Point

If oil is poured from one vessel into another, it flows in an arc of utter smoothness and silence. To the beholder there is something fascinating in the glasslike, motionless appearance of this rapid flow. Perhaps it reminds us of that aspect of time whose mysteries are even greater than those of the future and of the past—the infinitely short present, wedged in between these two infinitely long expanses extending in opposite directions. It is both our most immediate and our most intangible experience of reality. Now has no length, yet it is the only point in time at which what happens, happens and what changes, changes. It is past before we can even become aware of it, and yet, since every present moment is immediately followed by a new present moment, Now is our only direct experience of reality . . .

PAUL WATZLAWICK

Because I know that time is always time
And place is always and only place
And what is actual is actual only for one time
And only for one place
I rejoice that things are as they are . . .

T. S. ELIOT (EXCERPT FROM "ASH WEDNESDAY")

We want the spring to come and the winter to pass. We want whoever to call or not call, a letter, a kiss—we want more and more and then more of it. But there are moments, walking, when I catch a glimpse of myself in the window glass, say, the window of the corner video store, and I'm gripped by a cherishing so deep for my own blowing hair, chapped face, and unbuttoned coat that I'm speechless: I am living.

MARIE HOWE

God Is All

You ask me of God: to define the Nameless, to place in your palm the ultimate secret. Do not imagine that this is hidden somewhere far from you. The ultimate secret is the most open one. Here it is: God is All. . . .

Let me illustrate. It rained heavily during the night, and the street is thick with mud. I stopped to watch a group of little children playing with the mud. Oblivious to the damp, they made dozens of mud figures: houses, animals, towers. From their talk, it was clear that they imagined an identity for each. They gave the figures names and told their stories. For a while, the mud figures took on an independent existence. But they were all just mud. Mud was their source and mud was their substance. From the perspective of the children, their mud creations had separate selves. From the mud's point of view, it is clear such independence was an illusion—the creations were all just mud. . . .

When I look at the world, I do not see God. I see trees of various kinds, people of all types, houses, fields, lakes, cows, horses, chickens, and on and on. In this, I am like the children at play, seeing real figures and not simply mud. Where in all this is God? The question itself is misleading. God is not "in" this: God is this.

REB YERACHMIEL BEN YISRAEL

Soul of all souls, life of life—you are That

Seen and unseen, moving and unmoving—you are That

The road that leads to the City is endless;

Go without head or feet

And you'll already be there.

What else could you be?—you are That.

RUMI

It
Is
Near

When we look into our true experience of the world, we always come to a strange twoness. As humans we are more fragile than we can bear to know, buffeted by war and earthquake and also by the endless risings from within, by obsessions and longings, fear and anger. Yet at the same time, eternity presses itself upon us continually: it is near the way the hillside we stand on is near—forgotten, enormous, the source of nourishment and rest, thrusting up the grass spears where we lie down at ease. Both truths are always applicable: spirit brings its everlasting radiance, and soul helps us to receive the spirit's overwhelming gift.

Any authentic opening of mind embraces the greatness and smallness of who we are . . . Yet this experience happens entirely within the everyday . . . We awaken to the extraordinary in our lives—and the common flow does not change. We have our rhythm; we work, eat, drink, and talk together into the night. The catalyst becomes the only thing in the world, blossom or radio dial. Then we recollect the eternal, the hillside we stand upon and the source of blossoms and radio dials and cars and showers of rain among sun shafts. In our awakening, when the spirit is to the fore, what overtakes us, what shakes us til we wake, is stark, stark—pristine as a beech forest—and unarguably, blessedly real. Seen in the soul's light, eternity is voluptuous and an endless fusion with delight.

JOHN TARRANT

Absurdly Beautiful

Q: Osho, I feel life is very boring. What should I do?

A: As it is, you have already done enough. You have made life boring—some achievement! Life is such a dance of ecstasy and you have reduced it to boredom. You have done a miracle! What else do you want to do? You can't do anything bigger than this. Life and boring? You must have a tremendous capacity to *ignore* life.

. . . ignorance means the capacity to ignore. You must be ignoring the birds, the trees, the flowers, the people. Otherwise, life is tremendously beautiful, so *absurdly* beautiful, that if you can see it as it is you will never stop laughing. You will go on giggling—at least inside. Life is not boring, but *mind* is boring. And we create such a mind, such a strong mind, like a China Wall around ourselves, that it does not allow life to enter into us. It disconnects us from life. We become isolated, encapsulated, windowless . . .

Put aside your knowledge! And then look with empty eyes . . . And life is a *constant* surprise. And I am not talking about some divine life—the *ordinary* life is so extraordinary. In small incidents you will find the presence of God . . . Miss the present and you live in boredom. *Be* in the present and you will be surprised that there is boredom at all.

OSHO

The Way of No Effort

Poonjaji turned to me and asked me very directly, "When there is no past and no future, who are you?" I found myself looking inside to find out who I was, and in the moment of turning within there was what I can best describe as an explosion of silence. My body was alive and pulsating with energy, but the mind was totally silent. He repeated his question and I found myself saying, "I am." There was nothing else to say. "Very good," he said, his face lighting up. "Now, who are you when there is no 'I am'?"

There was another explosion inside after which my mouth said "Nothing." The word came from an unknown place, but I knew as soon as I uttered it that it was the correct answer. As the word came out, my body and mind seemed to explode again into an ever deeper silence. I had talked to him earlier about my mental habits and tendencies, mentioning that I could see very clearly that they were somehow obstructing my awareness. He looked at me and enquired, "Now, what is the nature of all those mental tendencies you were speaking about earlier?" The experience I was having gave me the answer. "They have no reality." "Good," he said. "Now you understand. This is where our work begins."

MURRAY FELDMAN[19]

This kind of account could easily generate "guru envy," leading some readers to jump on a plane to India. Notice how the pursuit of mystical experiences can keep us from seeing the miracle in the here and now.

---

[19]*See* Poonja in Sources and Permissions. From *Nothing Ever Happened, Volume 3,* by David Godman.

The Present Moment

Whatever one does [in meditation], whatever one tries to practice, is not aimed at achieving a higher state or at following some theory or ideal, but simply, without any object or ambition, trying to see what is here and now. One has to become aware of the present moment through such means as concentrating on the breathing . . . This is based on developing the knowledge of nowness, for each respiration is unique, it is an expression of *now*.

CHÖGYAM TRUNGPA

Meditation is not about getting to somewhere. Forget making progress. Forget higher states. Breathe in. Breathe out.

Happily
Ever
After

So imprudent are we that we wander in times that are not ours, and give no thought to the only time that does belong to us.

BLAISE PASCAL

It is only possible to live happily-ever-after on a day-to-day basis.

MARGARET BONNANO

Looking at everything as if for the first time reveals the commonplace to be utterly incredible, if only we can be alive to the newness of it.

RUTH BERNARD

Timelessness

On the first occasion (aged 8–10) I was in the garden, muddling about alone. A cuckoo flew over, calling. Suddenly, I experienced a sensation I can only describe as an effect that might follow the rotating of a kaleidoscope. It was a feeling of timelessness, not only that time stood still, that duration had ceased, but that I was myself outside time altogether. Somehow I knew I was part of eternity. And there was also a feeling of spacelessness. I lost all awareness of my surroundings. With this detachment I felt the intensest joy I had ever known, and yet with so great a longing—for what I did not know—that it was scarcely distinguishable from suffering . . .

The second occurred a good while after the first. It was an absolutely still day, flooded with sunshine. In the garden everything was shining, breathless, as if waiting expectant. Quite suddenly I felt convinced of the existence of God; as if I had only to put out my hand to touch Him. And at the same time there came that intensest joy and indescribable longing, as if of an exile, perhaps, for home. It seemed as if my heart were struggling to leap out of my body.

RERU ACCOUNT

This Is It!

Try: Reminding yourself from time to time: "This is it." See if there is anything at all that it cannot be applied to. Remind yourself that acceptance of the present moment has nothing to do with resignation in the face of what is happening. It simply means a clear acknowledgment that *what is happening is happening*. Acceptance doesn't tell you what to do. What happens next, what you choose to do, that has to come out of your understanding of this moment. You might try acting out of a deep knowing of "This is it." Does it influence how you choose to proceed or respond? Is it possible for you to contemplate that in a very real way, *this* may actually be the best season, the best moment of your life? If that was so, what would it mean for you?

JON KABAT-ZINN

"Keeping the mind that desires enlightenment is the wrong way . . . Only keep the great question. The great question means cutting off all thinking, becoming empty mind. So the mind that keeps the great question *is* enlightenment! You are already enlightened, but you don't know it. So after much hard training: ah, *this* is enlightenment! It is very easy. Can you see your eyes?" *"No."*

"You have no eyes? You *have* eyes. Can you grasp your mind?" *"No."* "You have no mind? It is the same. Can you see this cup? Can you hear my voice?" *"Yes."*

"This is your mind. My eyes can't see my eyes. To try to see my eyes is the wrong way. My mind can't understand my mind. So to try to understand my mind is the wrong way. If you cut off this mind, you will soon attain enlightenment. I can see this cup; so I have eyes. I can hear this sound; so I have mind. What am I? I am asking I. So there are no opposites. Having no opposites is the Absolute. So all thinking is cut off. Only don't know, only empty mind. This is my true self. It is very easy."

SEUNG SAHN

When you question intensely without turning to past experiences for answers, you are this "don't know mind."

229

No
Matter
What
It
Is

When I say the first line of the Lord's Prayer: "Our father who art in heaven . . ." I imagine this heaven as invisible, unenterable, but intimately close. There is nothing baroque about it, no swirling infinite space or stunning foreshortening. To find it—if one had the grace—it would only be necessary to lift up something as small and at hand as a pebble or a salt-cellar on the table . . .

"Thy kingdom come . . ." The difference is infinite between heaven and earth, yet the distance is minimal. Simone Weil wrote concerning this sentence: "Here our desire pierces through time to find eternity behind it and this happens when we know how to turn whatever happens, no matter what it is, into an object of desire."

JOHN BERGER

Everything Is All Right Forever

I was smelling flowers in the yard, and when I stood up I took a deep breath and the blood all rushed to my brain and I woke up dead on my back in the grass. I had apparently fainted, or died, for about sixty seconds. My neighbor saw me but thought I had just suddenly thrown myself on the grass to enjoy the sun. During that timeless moment of unconsciousness I saw the golden eternity. I saw heaven. In it nothing had ever happened, the events of a million years ago were just as phantom and ungraspable as the events of now or of a million years from now, or the events of the next ten minutes. It was perfect, the golden solitude, the golden emptiness, Something-Or-Other, something surely humble.

JACK KEROUAC

The Cabbage Sutra

I was practicing meditation in Benares, at a monastery situated right between a bus station and a train station. In the midst of this very noisy, urban location, there was one patch of garden, only a few square feet in size. One day I was sitting outside next to the few little tufts of grass and other things that grew there, and I noticed within the garden a single cabbage. In that instant, looking at the cabbage, I saw all of the forces of nature, with tentative form and tentative color, coming together in a certain configuration at a certain time—being born, growing old, decaying, dying. Distinctly appearing, yet without self-existence apart from the conditions that were coming together to form it. I also recognized that what I called my "self" was simply the forces of nature, with tentative form and color, coming together in a certain way at a certain time—having been born, growing old, decaying and dying . . . a constant flow of energy, with no entity of self beyond them or behind them. Sitting there, just looking, I became totally one with that cabbage.

SHARON SALZBERG

Are you looking for me? I am in the next seat.

My shoulder is against yours.

You will not find me in stupas,[20] not in Indian shrine rooms, nor in synagogues, nor in cathedrals:

Not in masses, nor kirtans.[21] not in legs winding around your own neck, nor in eating nothing but vegetables.

When you really look for me, you will see me instantly—

You will find me in the tiniest house of time.

Kabir says: Students, tell me, what is God?

He is the breath inside the breath.

KABIR

---

[20]Buddhist shrine.
[21]Chants, spiritual songs.

What
You
Are
Looking
Out
Of

I am the sole and final authority on one thing and one thing only, and that is what is right Here. You are the sole and final authority on what it's like where you are. You have inside information about what is sitting on your chair. I don't. So I am asking you about this thing on which you are the sole authority, which is your Reality, which is what you are looking out of. It's right where you are, totally obvious, totally available. This is not a sacred or peculiar kind of looking. It's simply looking in the right direction. We all look *out* very happily, but we are very bad at turning our attention around 180 degrees and looking *in*, at the place we are coming from. What you are looking out of is not perishable. There is nothing there to perish.

This is No-thing. I'm visibly No-thing, and where there's No-thing, there's no change. And where there's no change, there's no way of registering time. And where there's no way of registering time, time has not a chance. Time can't survive.

DOUGLAS E. HARDING

You are life and that is all you are. You are the infinite expression, and even as you ask the question, it is possible that you can see the answer in the question. Drop asking "why" and simply become totally involved in the absolutely wonderful miracle of life just as it is, right here, right now. Can you not see that whatever has just happened for you at this moment has never happened before and will never happen again? It is totally unique and fresh and innocent, and it is here and then it isn't. Isn't that great? And there, it's happened again, and you have just missed it because you want to ask another question about consciousness and its purpose for little old you. Just drop the head game and let it all be. The question and answer syndrome can be endless, and the mind often persuades us that the next answer that's on the next page might do it for us.

You don't need this imaginary person any longer, you know. This person that goes on and on and on asking questions, judging everything, calculating everything—just drop it. You have never needed that person, except that it brings you to this moment sitting here, hearing that you have never needed that person. Now drop it forever and simply allow life to happen without there being any illusory central datum or fixed point. Give up control and live in chaos. Fall in love with this, right here, right now . . .

TONY PARSONS

The Highest State

When I received the news of cancer, I understood, Oh, yes, what is required of me now is that I be fully present to each new experience as it comes and that I engage with it as completely as I can. I don't mean that I said this to myself. Nothing so conscious as that. I mean that my whole being turned, and looked, and moved toward the experience.

SANDY BOUCHER

Q: How to experience that Highest State?

M: There is no question of experiencing. You are that state only.

NISARGADATTA MAHARAJ

In the clarity of seeing what you are, how can there be a higher state?

[Hokusai (1760–1849) was a famous
Japanese artist.]

Hokusai says look carefully.
He says pay attention, notice.
He says keep looking, stay curious.
He says there is no end to seeing . . .

He says everything is alive—
shells, buildings, people, fish, mountains, trees.
Wood is alive. Water is alive.
Everything has its own life.
Everything lives inside us.
He says live with the world inside you.
He says it doesn't matter if you draw, or write books.
It doesn't matter if you saw wood, or catch fish . . .

It matters that you care. It matters that you feel.
It matters that you notice.
It matters that life lives through you.

ROGER KEYES

Immediate Reality

Since the synonyms of "mind," the labels we apply to it are countless, know it for what it really is. Know it experientially as the here and now. Compose yourself in the natural state of your mind's nature.

When at rest the mind is ordinary perception, naked and unadorned; when you gaze directly at it there is nothing to see but light; as Knowledge, it is brilliance and the relaxed vigilance of the awakened state; as nothing specific whatsoever, it is a secret fullness; it is the ultimacy of nondual radiance and emptiness.

It is not eternal, for nothing whatsoever about it has been proved to exist. It is not a void, for there is brilliance and wakefulness. It is not unity, for multiplicity is self-evident in perception. It is not multiplicity, for we know the one taste of unity. It is not an external function, for Knowledge is intrinsic to immediate reality.

LAMA SHABKAR[22]

 [22]From *The Flight of the Garuda* by Keith Dowman.

But if a man does well, God is really in him, and with him everywhere, on the streets and among people, just as much as in church, or a desert place, or a cell. If he really has God, and only God, then nothing disturbs him. Why? Because he has *only* God and thinks only God and everything is nothing but God to him. He discloses God in every act, in every place. The whole business of his person adds up to God. His actions are due only to him who is the author of them and not to himself, since he is merely the agent. . . .

When one takes God as he is divine, having the reality of God within him, God sheds light on everything. Everything will taste like God and reflect him. God will shine in him all the time.

MEISTER ECKHART

In Buddhism, the experience of nonduality is called the "one taste."

Life
Itself

At first, we try to look at our real nature as if it were an object. Then we understand that this attempt is doomed to failure. Next, we look at it as an absence of object, and at some point we understand that this search, too, is doomed to failure. Finally, we find our self in a state of not knowing, a state in which the mind has exhausted all of its possibilities and has no further place to go. We reach the understanding that the mind cannot grasp this luminous awareness which enlightens it, and we become still. We have to make acquaintance with this not knowing, to get used to this new dimension, to discover that it is not nothingness. This silent presence is not a mere absence of thoughts. It is alive. It is life itself.

FRANCIS LUCILLE

When there is no place to go, there is rest. There is peace.

Living Buddhas

There is a wonderful Buddha statue at the Metropolitan Museum. There are national-treasure bodhisattvas and many statues. They are wonderful, of course . . . But you are *living bodhisattvas,* each of you, living! Not bronze or wood. Sometime, something bad may happen. "Oh, I will pray to Buddha." No, no, no! There is no such Buddha. Realize this and every human being becomes wonderful . . . Open your own eyes! Don't think, "Oh, I am not yet enlightened. Some day I'll get enlightenment." From today, forget such! From the beginning, we are the Enlightened One. Believe this with definite faith . . . So with this mind, please let us bow to each other . . .

Without exception, each of you is a living Buddha . . . Without exception, okay?

SOEN NAKAGAWA

The Fact of What We Are

We don't have an escape route. And the whole process-oriented world is about an escape route. It's not about dealing with ourselves. It's about *not* facing ourselves by creating time, by creating process. If I can sit another retreat, or go to another seminar, or read another book, then I'll be able to fix everything. Of course it never works. We just get farther and farther away from the truth.

What if the world is only the fact of what we are? What happens if I am only anger and there is no escape? Now I have a different universe to explore, don't I? Now I get to explore what anger actually is. And I will discover that anger isn't what the psychiatrist described to me or what the workshop leader talked about. It's an occurrence that has certain qualities. It moves in certain parts of my body, and triggers certain kinds of feelings and memories, which all exist right now. Only now.

In this moment, we have stepped out of time, we're out of location, and we're in a transformational universe. At this moment, anger becomes energy. It's only when we blow that moment up into time and concept that it becomes anger. Then it is hooked into us in a way that makes it permanent.

STEVEN HARRISON

What are your imaginary escape routes? How do you use them to avoid what is happening now?

Shed Your Skin Completely

Don't look inside, don't seek outside. Don't try to quiet your thoughts or rest your body. Just know intimately; understanding intimately, cut off all at once, sit for a while and see. Though you may say there is no place in the four quarters to take a step and no place in the world to fit your body, ultimately you should not depend on the power of another.

When you see in this way, there are no skin, flesh, marrow, or bones set out for you; birth and death, coming and going, cannot change you. Having shed your skin completely, one true reality alone exists. It shines throughout all time, with no distinction of measure or time.

KEIZAN

Fragrance of Eternity

[Arthur Koestler had this experience while imprisoned in Spain.]

[It] swept over me like a wave. The wave had originated in an articulate verbal insight; but this evaporated at once, leaving in its wake only a wordless essence, a fragrance of eternity, a quiver of the arrow in the blue. I must have stood there for some minutes, entranced, with a wordless awareness that "this is perfect—perfect." . . . Then I was floating on my back in a river of peace, under bridges of silence. It came from nowhere and flowed nowhere. Then there was no river and no I. The I had ceased to exist . . . When I say "the I had ceased to exist," I refer to a concrete experience that is verbally as incommunicable as the feeling aroused by a piano concerto, yet just as real—only much more real. In fact, its primary mark is the sensation that this state is more real than any other one has experienced before.

ARTHUR KOESTLER

244

The whole universe
shatters into a hundred pieces.
In the great death
there is no heaven, no earth.

Once body and mind have turned over
there is only this to say:

Past mind cannot be grasped,
present mind cannot be grasped,
future mind cannot be grasped.

DOGEN

Why try and grasp the ungraspable when you
can die into the mystery right now?

No Path to Truth

One must die to all experience, because that which is accumulating, gathering, is the self, the "me," which is everlastingly seeking its own security, its own permanency and continuity. Any mind whose thought springs from this desire for self-perpetuation, the desire to attain, to succeed, whether in this world or in the next, is bound to be caught in illusion, and therefore in suffering. Whereas, if the mind begins to understand itself by being aware of its own activities, watching its own movements, its own reactions; if it is capable of dying psychologically to the desire to be secure so that it is free from the past, the past which is the accumulation of its own desires and experiences, the past which is the perpetuation of the "me," the self, the ego, then you will see that there are no paths to Truth at all, but a constant discovery from moment to moment.

After all, that which gathers, which hoards, which has continuity, is the "me," the self that knows suffering and is the outcome of time. It is this self-centered memory of the "me" and the "mine"—*my* possessions, *my* virtues, *my* qualities, *my* beliefs—which seeks security and desires to continue. Such a mind invents all these paths, which have no reality at all . . . When the mind can die psychologically to all things it has gathered for its own security, it is only then Reality comes into being.

J. KRISHNAMURTI

No Other Life but This

In eternity, there is indeed something true and sublime. But all these times and places and occasions are now and here. God himself culminates in the present moment, and will never be more divine in the lapse of all the ages.

Take time by the forelock. Now or never. You must live in the present, launch yourself on every wave, find your eternity in each moment. Fools stand on their island opportunities and look toward another land. There is no other land; there is no other life but this, or the like of this.

I wish to live ever as to derive my satisfactions and inspirations from the commonest events, every-day phenomena, so that what my senses hourly perceive, my daily walk, the conversation of my neighbors, may inspire me, and I may dream of no heaven but that which lies about me.

HENRY DAVID THOREAU

I Am Not Alone

One day when I was sitting quiet and feeling like a motherless child, which I was, it came to me: that feeling of being part of everything, not separate at all. I knew that if I cut a tree, my arm would bleed. And I laughed and I cried and I ran all around the house. I just knew what it was. In fact, when it happened, you can't miss it.

ALICE WALKER

I am part of the sun as my eye is part of me. That I am part of the earth my feet know perfectly, and my blood is part of the sea. There is not any of me that is alone and absolute except my mind, and we shall find that the mind has no existence by itself, it is only the glitter of the sun on the surface of the water.

D. H. LAWRENCE

Mistaken Identity

In August 2004 something happened that corrected a basic mistake in perception I'd lived with all my life. Prior to this occurrence I thought I was an individual consciousness experiencing an infinitely large, infinitely old, external universe of real objects. What I discovered, however, is that the consciousness I mistakenly perceived as belonging to an individual (Me), is in actuality God consciousness, the One consciousness, and that Me, the universe and everything in it are vague, ephemeral thought-forms appearing in and out of emptiness in a timeless, spaceless Now. It was a shattering revelation, but at the same time so obvious and self-evident I realized I'd known all along. I became un-fooled. A case of mistaken identity—very close to home—was resolved. There is *only* God consciousness. Here, where I am, there is consciousness. Therefore, I am That.

BART MARSHALL

The Moment of Looking

The first moment of looking into mind essence is called the "mindfulness of deliberate attention." The second moment, described as "free in the moment of seeing," does not mean one should look more, thinking, "Now, where is it? I had better look closer!" That creates more thinking. If you continue with, "Now, I see it! Where is it! I want to see it!" In this case you are just creating more thoughts within the state of buddha nature, a state that is by itself free from thought. . . .

They are all irrelevant thoughts. In the moment of seeing allow for a continuity free from thought. Simply rest freely in that.

TULKU URGYEN RINPOCHE

Stop constructing. Start seeing. Just look now and let it be.

No Such Thing as Enlightenment

There's no such thing as enlightenment. It's a completely extraneous pursuit. To realize conclusively that the Buddha Mind you have from your parents innately is unborn and marvelously illuminating—*that's* enlightenment. *Not* realizing this makes you deluded. Since the Original Buddha Mind is unborn, it functions without thoughts of delusion or thoughts of wanting to be enlightened. As soon as you think of wanting to be enlightened, you leave the place of the Unborn and go counter to it. Because the Buddha Mind is unborn, it has no thoughts at all. Thoughts are the source of delusion. When thoughts are gone, delusion vanishes too. And once you've stopped being deluded, talking about wanting to attain "enlightenment" certainly is useless, don't you agree?

When you try to stop your rising thoughts, you create a duality between the mind that does the stopping and the mind that's being stopped, so you'll never have peace of mind. Just have faith that thoughts don't originally exist, but only arise and cease temporarily in response to what you see and hear, without any actual substance of their own.

BANKEI

Many students of meditation are at war with their thoughts and feelings. This conflict will never end as long as we see that which is arising now as something to be eradicated.

251

A Quiet Space

[Toni Packer wrote this following the attack on the World Trade Center.]

Someone asked for a few words of advice for dealing with the torrent of feelings, emotions, and confusions that are coming up in the wake of the horrendous explosions outside and in that shook many of us to the roots.

If possible, can we find a quiet moment in a quiet space in the midst of all the noise, agitation and confusion, a quiet spot in the eye of sadness and grief, pain, anger, and rage, the urge for revenge, and the longing for security to end all suffering? Can we listen silently to the contractions of fear, anger and the throbbing of longing for safety? . . .

Can we come back time and time again, with infinite patience, to what is actually taking place *right now*, this very moment—the sadness and grief paining heart and mind, fear knotting one's stomach and guts, anger making the heart pound faster, driving blood to the head, and also hear the sound of rain, motor noises around us, the brightness and darkness of the room, the sky, the smell in the air—not just the reactions to all of this, but simply perceiving sounds and sights and the feel of what is actually taking place?

TONI PACKER

Come to Your Senses

There is only one Truth
and as you go looking for it
through a forest of seeking
be careful lest you bump into a tree.
That lump on your head
may remind you that
everything is God.

You are like a forest dweller
looking for the forest.
What am I to do?

Listen friend
each crackling leaf beneath your feet
is a personal invitation
to come to your senses.

Has it ever occurred to you
that you are seeking God
with His eyes?

ADYASHANTI

Every sound you hear is a personal invitation to
come to your senses, to be home here.

The Ecstasy of Not Being Anybody

Enlightenment
is life without a future,
liberation from the pretense of safety.

Without a future, where did the past go?

It is the end of the known,
and the endless exploration of the Unknown.

It is the end of the struggle
to be anybody or get anything.
It is the end of looking for anything.
It is the end of trying to become anything.
It is the end of trying to hold onto anything.
It is the end of trying to make something happen,
or not happen.

What a relief!

SCOTT MORRISON

Rigpa

[Rigpa][23] is the real condition, innate suchness.[24]
Actually, it is very neat to call it "ordinary mind."
Ordinary mind in this sense does not refer to the
mind of an ordinary person. It refers to a state of mind that is
totally unspoiled, that is uncorrupted by any kind of disturbing
emotions, conceptual thoughts or fixations.

We can call it ordinary mind, self-existing awareness or buddha-
nature—whatever we call *it*, that "it" is always present in ourselves. Unfortunately we usually fail to recognize what is already
present as our own basic nature. No one else can recognize this
intrinsic self-existing wakefulness for us. The very moment we
abandon all conceptual activity such as accepting or rejecting,
keeping or sending off, judging or evaluating, ordinary mind, self-
existing awareness is naturally present.

CHOKYI NYIMA RINPOCHE

When there is recognition of the real condition
of things, the extraordinary becomes ordinary
and the ordinary, extraordinary.

[23]*Rigpa*—Intrinsic Awareness, true nature.
[24]In Buddhism, "suchness" is often used to denote true being or essence.

Forever
Astonished

When he [Zorba] writes, this ignorant workman breaks his pens in his impetuosity. Like the first men to cast off their monkey skins, or like the great philosophers, he is dominated by the basic problems of mankind. He lives them as if they were immediate and urgent necessities. Like the child, he sees everything for the first time. He is forever astonished and wonders why and wherefore. Everything seems miraculous to him, and each morning when he opens his eyes he sees trees, sea, stones and birds, and is amazed.

"What is this miracle?" he cries. "What are these mysteries called: trees, sea, stones, birds?"

NIKOS KAZANTZAKIS

Another exercise: When you wake up tomorrow morning, see everything as miracle, as mystery.

[Thoreau] found, by opening his eyes, that life provides everything necessary for man's peace and enjoyment—one has only to make use of what is there . . . "Life is bountiful," he seems to be saying all the time. *"Relax!* Life is here, all about you, not there, not over the hill."

He found Walden. But Walden is everywhere, if the man himself is there. Walden has become a symbol. It should become a reality. Thoreau himself has become a symbol. But he was only a man, let us not forget that. By making him a symbol, by raising memorials to him, we defeat the very purpose of his life. Only by living our own lives to the full can we honor his memory. We should not try to imitate him but to surpass him. Each of us has a totally different life to lead. We should not strive to become like Thoreau, or even like Jesus Christ, but to become what we are in truth and in essence. That is the message of every great individual and the whole meaning of being an individual. To be anything less is to move nearer to nullity.

HENRY MILLER

Being the Present Moment

Everything that happens in the present moment is necessary.

The crux of man's dilemma lies in the concept of time. While chasing his mythical happiness of the future, man has no time to enjoy the present moment. And actually there is no such thing as the present because by the time one thinks of it, it has already become the past. Therefore, what is vital is not *thinking* about the present but actually *being* that present moment—and that is nothing other than enlightenment.

In order to understand this strange, unknown, starkly inevitable thing called death we must first understand life. What we must find out is *what we are now*. To die *now* to every moment and every experience is the death that is ETERNITY ITSELF.

RAMESH S. BALSEKAR

Everything that happens is necessary. Now that's an interesting koan! Just for fun, try using this phrase for an entire day and see what happens.

My Peace Is There

my way is in the sand flowing
between the shingle and the dune
the summer rain rains on my life
on me my life harrying fleeing
to its beginning to its end

my peace is there in the receding mist
when I may cease from treading these long shifting thresholds
and live the space of a door
that opens and shuts.

SAMUEL BECKETT

Joy

When I was nine and living in Tripoli, Libya, I had an experience of joy, thirty seconds or so, that I count as the real beginning of my conscious life . . .

It was probably seven thirty when I stood at the top of a low cliff by a set of wooden stairs. The tranquility of the Mediterranean—a cleaner, brighter sea then—seemed inseparable from a sweetness in the air and the sound of small waves breaking. The beach of white sand was deserted. It was all mine. The space which separated me from what I saw sparkled with significance. Everything I looked at—yesterday's footprints in the sand, an outcrop of rock, the wooden rail beneath my hand—seemed overpoweringly unique, etched in light, and somehow to be aware of itself, to "know." At the same time, everything belonged together, and that unity was knowing too and seemed to say, Now you've seen us. I felt myself dissolving into what I saw. I was no longer a son or a schoolboy or a Wolf Cub. And yet I felt my individuality intensely, as though for the first time. I was coming into being. I murmured something like, "I am me," or "This is me." Even now, I sometimes find this kind of formulation useful.

IAN MCEWAN

A ccept what the present brings and live in that. If one is not established in the present, then one is nowhere and nothing is possible.

RODNEY COLLIN

Eternity isn't some later time. Eternity isn't even a long time. Eternity has nothing to do with time. Eternity is that dimension of here and now that all thinking in temporal times cuts off. And if you don't get it here, you won't get it anywhere . . . the experience of eternity right here and now, in all things, whether thought of as good or as evil, is the function of life. This is it.

JOSEPH CAMPBELL

In Buddhist practice, bring everything, whatever it is, from all directions, into the present moment, then drop the present. Then time vanishes . . . Timelessness in Buddhism has to do with the dissolving of conceptual mind, letting go of concepts. In the moment of letting go of concepts, you are already in timelessness.

TSOKNYI RINPOCHE

God Was London (excerpt)

In a dreary evening
From a window at my hospital
I raised my eyes up . . . up . . . ,
To His grey and wide sky.
I felt Him in my whole self.
His overpowering strength
Enthralled my mind and my body
Enthroned in my heart
Because God was in the Thames
Flowering gloriously.
God was in the Big Ben
Standing All Mighty.
God was in the Westminster Bridge
So hilariously . . .
And He was in my tears
So bitter and yet so soothingly
So comfortingly, lovingly
That I somehow knew.
Knew He was in me
Knew He was in London
Knew that God was London.

RERU POEM

262

In the Smallest Detail

When one becomes disentangled from the grasp of the discriminatory mind, a different kind of seeing is free to emerge. As a teenager, I unconsciously adopted the belief that some subjects deserved to be photographed more than others. I didn't have a list in mind of what I thought was acceptable or not, but after a while I noticed that I always seemed to photograph the same cluster of subjects, family, friends, animals, landscapes, or sports events.

One day I had a shocking experience. Someone who had taken a picture of a door won the first prize in a photography contest. I could not believe that such a common subject could be judged worthy of a prize. Of course, that was before I tried to photograph a door. I had no idea how difficult it would be to construct an image that would make an ordinary door interesting. The incident provoked me to pay closer attention to the ordinary. Over time, I began to appreciate, in photography and in my everyday life, a remark made long ago by the ancient Taoist Lao-Tzu: "The secret of the Tao is found in the smallest detail of the ordinary day."

PHILIPPE L. GROSS

Try this: go and explore this perfectly ordinary day, without a story.

Letters from God

I hear and behold God in every object, yet understand God not in the least,

Nor do I understand who there can be more wonderful than myself.

Why should I wish to see God better than this day?

I see something of God each hour of the twenty-four, and each moment then,

In the faces of men and women I see God, and in my own face in the glass,

I find letters from God dropt in the street, and every one is sign'd by God's name,

And I leave them where they are, for I know wheresoe'er I go,

Others will punctually come for ever and ever.

WALT WHITMAN

In his eulogy, Robert Ingersoll said of Whitman: "He had the courage to meet all, and was great enough and splendid enough to harmonize all and to accept all there is of life as a divine melody."

Y ou can practice mindfulness, because there is forgetfulness; but you cannot practice aware- ness, because there is only awareness. In mindfulness, you pay attention to the present moment. You try to "be here now." But pure aware- ness is the present state of awareness before you try to do *anything* about it. Trying to "be here now" requires a future moment in which you will then be mindful; but pure awareness is this moment before you try anything. You are already aware; you are already enlightened . . .

It's like peering into the window of a department store and see- ing a vague figure staring back at you. You let the figure come into focus, and with a shock realize that it's your own reflection in the window. The entire world, according to these traditions, is nothing but the reflection of your own Self, reflected in the mirror of your own awareness. See? You are already looking right at it.

KEN WILBER

One World at a Time

[A description of Henry David Thoreau as he lay dying in 1862.]

"I never saw a man dying with so much pleasure and peace," was the remark made afterwards by one of his visitors; which recalls to mind the last words of Thoreau's last letter: "I am enjoying existence as much as ever, and regret nothing."

Several of his utterances on these occasions were very characteristic. When Channing, the faithful and intimate companion of his walks and studies, hinted at the weary change that had now come over his life, and how "solitude began to peer out curiously from the dells and wood roads," he whispered in reply, "It is better some things should end." He said to Alcott that he "should leave the world without a regret." Not in these last weary months of suffering did he lose his shrewd humor and native incisiveness of speech. "Well, Mr. Thoreau, we must all go," said a well-meaning visitor, who thought to comfort the dying man by the ordinary platitudes. "When I was a boy," answered Thoreau, "I learnt that I must die, so I am not disappointed now; death is as near to you as it is to me." When asked whether he "had made peace with God," he replied that "he had never quarreled with him." He was invited by another acquaintance to enter into a religious conversation concerning the next world. "One world at a time," was the quiet retort.

HENRY S. SALT

Death is always near. Make your peace on each breath.

That
Is
Sufficient

Actually there is not a moment that you are not realized. It happens now with you! Why now? Because it is happening now! Only your mind cannot recognize it. . . .

That is sufficient! Does the ripe apple think, when will I fall? The moment it says: "When?" "When?" believe me, then it will never fall! Never ask when! When means future. Then your mind jumps to the future.

You recognize: I am here. She is here. He is here. Let me be silent! Something is said here. Listening is here. Let me just listen! That is all. Let me say nothing. Mind, keep quiet! Just listen. That is sufficient. Existence will take care of you.

DR. VIJAI S. SHANKAR

The Holy Grail

The search may begin with a restless feeling, as if one were being watched. One turns in all directions and sees nothing. Yet one senses that there is a source for this deep restlessness; and the path that leads there is not a path to a strange place, but the path home. ("But you *are* home," cries the Witch of the North. "All you have to do is wake up.") The journey is hard, for the secret place *where we have always been* is overgrown with thorns and thickets of "ideas," of fears and defenses, prejudices and repressions. The holy grail is what Zen Buddhists call our own "true nature"; each man is his own savior after all.

PETER MATTHIESSEN

Who is making this journey so hard and who can make it easy? Who can end this search right now?

A monk asked Wei-kuan: "Where is Tao?"[25]

Kuan: "Right before us."

Monk: "Why don't I see it?"

Kuan: "Because of your egotism, you cannot see it."

Monk: "If I cannot see it because of my egotism, does your reverence see it?"

Kuan: "As long as there is 'I and you,' this complicates the situation and there is no seeing Tao."

Monk: "When there is neither 'I' nor 'you' is it seen?"

Kuan: "When there is neither 'I' nor 'you,' who is here to see it?"

WEI-KUAN

Without Asking Anything

[25]*Tao*—the Way, Essence, Truth—from Chinese Taoist tradition. Often used in Chinese Buddhism in place of *Dharma*.

If we are honest with ourselves, we realize that we persistently view the present as a means towards an end. According to conventional reality, the events of the present moment are the result of causes in the past. What we do with those results, how we react to them, in turn sows the seeds of future effects. This is the world we live in. We see causes in the past; experience the effects of them in the present; respond or react to these effects; and so convert them into new causes of future events.

When we look at life this way, we are trapped. We don't really see the world—all we see is how it is for *me*, what it means to *me*, and what *I* have to get from it. In this way, the present is a commodity that we consume, manipulate and exploit; something we can use now to profit from it in the future. Even when we talk about inner work—seeing clearly, inquiring, investigating and seeing into things—our mind wants something from it. What would it mean to look at life without asking anything from it— even if for only a moment?

CHRISTOPHER TITMUSS

On the Ground

Usually people interested in spiritual development think in terms of the importance of mind, that mysterious, high and deep thing that we have decided to learn about. But strangely enough the profound and transcendental are to be found in the factory.

CHÖGYAM TRUNGPA

On another occasion, over coffee, a woman said it was difficult to mix Zen with being a housewife. She felt she was trying to climb a ladder, but for every step up she'd go down two. "Forget the ladder," Suzuki told her. "In Zen everything is right here on the ground."

SHUNRYU SUZUKI

In the Jungle

Lost in the awe at the beauty around me, I must have slipped into a state of heightened awareness. It is hard—impossible, really—to put into words the moment of truth that suddenly came upon me then. Even the mystics are unable to describe their brief flashes of spiritual ecstasy. It seemed to me, as I struggled afterward to recall the experience, that self was utterly absent: I and the chimpanzees, the earth and trees and air, seemed to merge, to become one with the spirit power of life itself. The air was filled with a feathered symphony, the evensong of birds. I heard new frequencies in their music and also in the singing insects' voices—notes so high and sweet I was amazed. Never had I been so intensely aware of the shape, the color of the individual leaves, the varied patterns of the veins that made each one unique. Scents were clear as well, easily identifiable: fermenting, overripe fruit; waterlogged earth; cold, wet bark; the damp odor of chimpanzee hair, and yes, my own too. And the aromatic scent of young, crushed leaves was almost overpowering.

JANE GOODALL

He is loved, I said to myself in front of the drawing of olive trees, because for him the act of drawing or painting was a way of discovering and demonstrating why *he* loved so intensely what he was looking at, and what he looked at during the eight years of his life as a painter (yes only eight) belonged to everyday life . . . [For him[the chair is a chair, not a throne. The boots have been worn by walking. The sunflowers are plants, not constellations. The postman delivers letters. The irises will die. And from this nakedness of his, which his contemporaries saw as naivety or madness, came his capacity to love, suddenly at any moment, what he saw in front of him. Picking up pen or brush, he then strove to *achieve* that love. Lover-painter affirming the toughness of an everyday tenderness we all dream of in our better moments and instantly recognize when it is framed.

JOHN BERGER, WRITING ON VINCENT VAN GOGH

Things
of
the
Past

Although researchers have failed to find evidence for a single "time organ" in the brain, in the manner of, say, the visual cortex, it may be that future work will pin down those brain processes responsible for our sense of temporal passage. It is possible to imagine drugs that could suspend the subject's impression that time is passing. Indeed, some practitioners of meditation claim to be able to achieve such mental states naturally.

And what if science were able to explain away the flow of time? Perhaps we would no longer fret about the future or grieve for the past. Worries about death might become as irrelevant as worries about birth. Expectation and nostalgia might cease to be part of human vocabulary. Above all, the sense of urgency that attaches to so much of human activity might evaporate. No longer would we be slaves to Henry Wadsworth Longfellow's entreaty to "act, act in the living present," for the past, present and future would literally be things of the past.

PAUL DAVIES

Hallaj: Don't be afraid nor try to join me. For your way is yours, don't imitate mine. You'll find your way.

Ibn Ata: When, master?

Hallaj: When in a crowd or alone you perceive impatience disappearing, and you know just where you are and where you're meant to be.

Ibn Ata: Where is that, master?

Hallaj: Anywhere. You will know your action. You are present there, not thinking of somewhere else you ought to be.

HERBERT MASON (FROM *THE DEATH OF AL-HALLAJ*)

Listen
Quietly

When Zen Master Shen-ts'an was preparing to depart this life, he shaved his head, bathed himself, and had the temple bell sounded to summon the congregation and announce his departure.

Then he asked, "Brothers, do you understand the voiceless *samadhi*?"[26]

Those assembled answered, "No, we do not."

The master said, "Listen quietly without cherishing any ideas." With the congregation on the very tiptoe of expectation that they would hear about the voiceless *samadhi*, Master Shen-ts'an withdrew from the world.

SHEN-TS'AN

Listen now, don't try to understand.

[26]*samadhi*—meditative absorption, a deep meditational state of awareness or union.

Even the event we remember as "turning-to-this-page" can't be found. It doesn't exist **Now**. There's no Real event corresponding to the phrase "turning-to-this-page." It's merely a relative event, a concept, tucked away in memory and probably soon to be forgotten. It's not **Now**. Not as you read this. Not in Reality. So, where *is* "turning-to-this-page?" How did we get **Here** if it isn't Real? How did we get to this dynamic event which is **Now**? The Truth is, we didn't *get* **Here**. **Now** is where we've *always* been.

Our common sense may have us think that what's being discussed here is nonsense—or, at least, just a play with words which points to nothing more than vague abstractions which have no connection with the Real World. But in this common-sense assessment, we're completely turned around. It's because we habitually react in this way that we remain confused and never seem to find our way to Truth.

On the contrary, what's being indicated here is immediate and Real. It's our conceptual reality, where we spend virtually all our intellectual life, which is utterly abstract. And, with common sense, we habitually confuse our abstractions with Reality. What we commonly call "now," unlike the past and the future, is Absolute and not relative at all. It's **Now**. **Now** holds both past and future and "takes place" outside of time. It's for this reason we can't hold **Now** in concept . . .

STEVE HAGEN

Holding Silence's Hand

[Twenty years ago, Marc Lerner contracted multiple sclerosis, rendering him legally blind. During the Passover season, he writes daily poems.]

Most people walk through life along the path
of their thoughts and conditioning,
but my illness stole that away from me,
forcing me to be led by a silent guide into the moment.
It is as if I hold Silence's hand and enter the unknown
without the protection of thinking,
discovering things in the moment ,
only my deepest wisdom knows.
My illness may have crippled me to live in society,
but in every moment it shifts me beyond thinking
where my breath seems to tenderly touch God in silence.

MARC LERNER

It could happen any time, tornado,
earthquake, Armageddon. It could happen.
Or sunshine, love, salvation.

It could, you know. That's why we wake
and look out—no guarantees
in this life.

But some bonuses, like morning,
like right now, like noon,
like evening.

WILLIAM STAFFORD

Inside and Outside

If those who lead you say to you,
"See, the kingdom is in the sky,"
then the birds of the sky will precede you.
If they say to you, "It is in the sea,"
then the fish will precede you.
Rather, the kingdom is inside of you, and it is outside of you.
When you come to know yourselves, then you will become known,
and you will realize that it is you
who are the sons of the living father.

JESUS

No inside. No outside. This is all your kingdom.

What We Already Know

Most of us have a strong attachment to our story of what happened in the past, and often don't recognize how powerfully this story affects our lives. We are not only attached to memories of the good times, but also to memories of the bad times. There is a fear that if we let go of it, we will all be less interesting or that we won't know who we are anymore—that something important about us will die. In order to move into our full potential as human beings, there has to be a letting go of what we already know. Most people hold on to what they know for fear they won't survive. What keeps us stuck in the same old stories is that we never let them complete themselves. Waking up, the ability to live in the moment, is a dying of the old, the old way in which we perceive our lives. There has to be a stepping out of our attachment to the past in order to discover who we are in this moment.

ARIEL AND SHYA KANE

What Are You Saving Yourself For?

Are you really in your hands, or do you move them from a distance? Are you present in your cells, inhabiting and filling your body? If you aren't in your body, what significance is there in your experience this moment? Are you preparing, so that you can be here in the future? Are you setting up conditions by saying to yourself, "When such and such happens I'll have time, I'll be here"? If you are not here, what are you saving yourself for?

Regardless of the stories you tell yourself, at this moment, this very moment, there is only this moment, here, now. Nothing else exists. For your direct experience, only the here and now is relevant. Only now is real. And it is always like that. At each moment, only that moment exists. So we need to ask why we put ourselves on hold, waiting for the right time, waiting for the right circumstances to rise in the future. Maybe the right time will never come. Maybe the conditions you have in mind will never come together for you. When will you begin to exist then? When will you begin to be here, to live? Regardless of the ideas about past and future that dominate your experience, right at this moment only this moment exists, and only this moment has any significance for you . . .

A. H. ALMAAS

[In the film *American Beauty*, Lester, on the verge of death, delivers this monologue.]

It's hard to stay mad, when there's so much beauty in the world. Sometimes I feel like I'm seeing it all at once, and it's too much, my heart fills up like a balloon that's about to burst . . . And then I remember to relax, and stop trying to hold on to it, and then it flows through me like rain and I can't feel anything but gratitude for every single moment of my stupid little life . . .

LESTER IN *AMERICAN BEAUTY* (ALAN BALL, SCREENWRITER)

Right at Hand

Awakening is the recovery of that awesome freedom into which we were born but for which we have substituted the pseudo-independence of a separate self. No matter how much it frightens us, no matter how much we resist it, such freedom is right at hand. It may break into our lives at any time, whether we seek it or not, enabling us to glimpse a reality that is simultaneously more familiar and more elusive than anything we have ever known, in which we find ourselves both profoundly alone and profoundly connected to everything. Yet the force of habit is such that suddenly it is lost again and we are back to unambiguous normality.

Through counteracting this force of habit, dharma practice[27] has two objectives: to let go of self-centered craving so that our lives become gradually more awake; and to be receptive to the sudden eruption of awakening into our lives at any moment. Awakening is both a linear process of freedom that is cultivated over time *and* an ever present possibility of freedom. The central path is both a track with a beginning and an end *and* the formless potentiality at the very center of experience.

STEPHEN BATCHELOR

> Waking up encompasses every moment of your life and is only realized now, never in an imagined future. Gradual and sudden disappear in this moment.

[27]Refers to Buddhist practices such as meditation, following precepts, etc.

This Water

Oren Lyons was the first Onondagan[28] to enter college. When he returned to his reservation for his first vacation, his uncle proposed a fishing trip on the lake. Once he had his nephew in the middle of the lake where he wanted him, he began to interrogate him. "Well, Oren," he said, "you've been to college; you must be pretty smart now from all they've been teaching you. Let me ask you a question. Who are you?" Taken aback by the question, Oren fumbled for an answer. "What do you mean, who am I? Why, I'm your nephew, of course." His uncle rejected his answer and repeated his question. Successively, the nephew ventured that he was Oren Lyons, an Onondagan, a human being, a man, a young man, all to no avail. When his uncle had reduced him to silence and he asked to be informed as to who he was, his uncle said, "Do you see that bluff over there? Oren, you *are* that bluff. And that giant pine on the other shore? Oren, you are that pine. And this water that supports our boat? You are this water."

HUSTON SMITH

So, who are you?

---

[28]Native American tribe.

To
Live
Abundantly

We get caught in the belief that this is not quite it . . .

DASARATH

If you want to know what eternity means, it is no further than this very moment. If you fail to catch it in this present moment, you will not get it, however many times you are reborn in hundreds of thousands of years.

SEPPO

A religious act is performed out of good motivation with sincere thought for the benefit of others. Religion is here and now in our daily lives. If we lead that life for the benefit of the world, this is the hallmark of a religious life. This is my simple religion. No need for temples. No need for complicated philosophy. Your own mind, your own heart is the temple; your philosophy is simple kindness.

THE DALAI LAMA

Only when we are no longer afraid do we begin to live in every experience, painful or joyous, to live in gratitude for every moment, to live abundantly.

DOROTHY THOMPSON

Simple and Easy

All that effort, all that energy, to annihilate the ego . . . and it's not there in the first place. There's nothing to strive for and there's nothing to get rid of. We need only to stop creating the self in our minds in each moment. To be in the moment free of concept, free of image, free of clinging. To be simple and easy. There's no struggle or tension in that invisibility, in that effortlessness.

Q: How can we make an effort without striving?

A: The effort is exactly to be free of striving; settling back to be mindful in the moment. Some of you may have experienced, in the growth of awareness, not being caught up in projections or concepts. When the mind is in that space, there is nothing to do. When you sit down, it's just sitting, and you are effortlessly aware of whatever is happening.

Q: What about planning that has to be done?

A: The planning mind is happening in the moment. Be aware of the planning mind as an expression of the present moment. To be just with what's happening, using the thought process and the whole conceptual framework in dealing with the world, but staying grounded by realizing it's all just now. To act without attachment to the fruits of the action.

JOSEPH GOLDSTEIN

At
the
Core

The show is over when we realize it is a show. When we see clearly that the story is a story, that the storyteller is a story, that the "me" is a story, then the curtain falls. The applause is deafening only in its absolute silence.

We have discovered that at the core of our existence is not a center, but, like the proverbial onion, as we strip away each layer, in the end we come to nothing. There is no one at the core. We may use the word nothing here, but it is not the word that is at our core. We could as easily say that at our center is everything. We could say it is love, or consciousness, or a vast field of awareness in which everything arises, including the very idea of a separate self.

What is at the core is not in language, it is not a subject or object, it is not in thought or word of any kind. It is not divided, so it cannot be objectified. It is not possessed, so it cannot be mine.

Here, at last, we find life itself. Being without doing, a script gone silent, the greatest story ever untold.

STEVEN HARRISON

A Living Slice

We spend much of our time caught up in memories of the past or looking ahead to the future, full of worries and plans. The breath has none of that "other-timeness." When we truly observe the breath, we are automatically placed in the present. We are pulled out of the morass of mental images and into a bare experience of the here-and-now. In this sense, breath is a living slice of reality. A mindful observation of such a miniature model of life itself leads to insights that are broadly applicable to the rest of our experience.

HENEPOLA GUNARATANA

Awareness may be easier than you imagine. Each day you breathe in and out thousands of times. Simply notice your breath.

Now
or
Never

To understand the immeasurable, the mind must be extraordinarily quiet, still; but if I think I am going to achieve stillness at some future date, I have destroyed the possibility of stillness. It is now or never. That is a very difficult thing to understand, because we are all thinking of heaven in terms of time.

Nothing is essential for stillness but stillness itself; it is its own beginning and its own end. No essentials bring it about, for it is. No means can ever lead to stillness. It is only when stillness is something to be gained, achieved, that the means become essential. If stillness is to be bought, then the coin becomes important; but the coin, and that which it purchases, are not stillness. Means are noisy, violent, or subtly acquisitive, and the end is of like nature, for the end is in the means. If the beginning is silence, the end is also silence. There are no means to silence; silence is when noise is not. Noise does not come to an end through the further noise of effort, of discipline, of austerities, of will. See the truth of this, and there is silence.

J. KRISHNAMURTI

Perfect in Every Moment

I remember one morning. Getting up at dawn. There was such a sense of possibility. We were going to do everything. Do you know that feeling? I remember thinking: "This is the beginning of happiness." That's what I thought. "So this is the feeling. This is where it starts. And of course there'll always be more." It never occurred to me: it wasn't the beginning. It *was* happiness. It was the moment, right then.

CLARISSA IN *THE HOURS* (DAVID HARE, SCREENWRITER)

These roses under my window make no reference to former roses or to better ones; they are for what they are; they exist with God today. There is no time to them. There is simply the rose; it is perfect in every moment of its existence. Before a leaf-bud has burst, its whole life acts; in the full-blown flower there is no more; in the leafless root there is no less. Its nature is satisfied, and it satisfies nature, in all moments alike.

RALPH WALDO EMERSON

We are here and it is now. Further than that, all human knowledge is moonshine.

H. L. MENCKEN

Just See What the Buddha Saw

I don't say you need to practice some advanced form of meditation. Just see what the Buddha saw. This mind is buddha mind.

"Buddha mind," "all beings," "wisdom," and "defilement," the names of these things are different, but actually they are one body. You should each recognize your miraculous mind. Its essence is apart from temporary or everlasting. Its nature is without pollution or purity. It is clear and perfect. Common people and sages are the same. This mind reaches everywhere without limit . . . If you can comprehend this, then there is nothing that you lack.

SHI TOU

Many spiritual practitioners assume they must reach an advanced level of meditation in order to realize the highest truth. Notice how this assumption can keep us from simple clear seeing.

292

It Became Alive

It was during one of those visits that I experienced a moment of the purest joy, and, I think, came closer to ecstasy than ever before or since. We were in the British Museum, in front of a three-thousand year old Egyptian sculpture, which [my friend] Dante particularly loved. He thought it was the work of a great spiritual master and contained deep wisdom, which one needed to absorb. We had visited it many times in the past, and it had become very familiar to me. But now, suddenly, I realized that I had never really seen it before. For a moment, I don't know how long, it became alive, perfect, full of beauty and wisdom, radiating compassion and peace. For the first time in my life, I felt totally focused and still. At that instant I knew what it meant to "find God" . . . In that one single moment out of time, I had been given a glimpse of a reality, which could never *not be*, a pledge of eternity at the core of all being.

IRMA ZALESKI

We do not see things as they are—we see things as we are. When I drop my story, everything is fresh and new; I see as if for the first time.

Marvelous
Splendor

Sitting one day in his room, his eyes fell upon a burnished pewter dish, which reflected the sunshine with such marvelous splendor that he fell into an inward ecstasy. It seemed to him as if he could now look into the principles and deepest foundations of things. He believed that it was only a fancy, and in order to banish it from his mind he went out upon the green. But here, he remarked that he gazed into the very heart of things, the very herbs and grass, and that actual nature harmonized with what he had inwardly seen. He said nothing of this to anyone, but praised and thanked God in silence.

ACCOUNT OF THE FAMOUS PROTESTANT MYSTIC JACOB BOEHME'S EXPERIENCE AT THE AGE OF 25 IN THE YEAR 1600.

For a Heartbeat

[Six-year-old Frederick was with his mother on a picnic. He snuck off by himself and heard an orchestra playing.]

I saw my chance to escape across a narrow stream, and found myself in a sun-drenched meadow. I lay down in fragrant, swaying grasses, tall enough to make me invisible, listening to the piano's arpeggios, the cello's moaning in the distance.

Then, suddenly, there was a loud zooming close to my ear. I was terrified. A big velvety bee circled around my head, almost touched it. But then it ignored me to land on the purple flower that was so close by that it looked huge and vague, and started to suck.

At that precise instant it happened: suddenly all my fright evaporated, but with it the bee, the sun, the grass, and I disappeared. Sunlight, sky, grasses, bee, and I merged, fused, yet somehow remaining sun, sky, grass, bee, and I. It may have lasted for a heartbeat, an hour, or a year; it was timeless. Then, just as abruptly, the grass was grass again and I was I again, but filled with indescribable bliss.

FREDERICK FRANCK

Only a Matter of Seeing

Yin-tsung also asked "How is the legacy of the Fifth Zen Patriarch demonstrated and transmitted?"

I said, "There is no demonstration or transmission; it is only a matter of seeing [original] nature, not a matter of meditation and liberation."

Yin-tsung asked, "Why is it not a matter of meditation and liberation?"

I said, "Because these two things are not Buddhism; Buddhism is a non-dualistic teaching."

HUI-NENG

After years of meditation and spiritual practice, I discovered this teaching and was astonished. Here, the founder of Chinese Zen states that Zen has nothing to with meditation, transmission, or liberation. It is only about seeing.

Behold, It Is Very Good

[While on vacation in Thailand, John Wren-Lewis was poisoned during an attempted robbery. He fell into a coma, and when he awoke days later, found his state of awareness altered.]

It is all still here, both the shining dark void and the experience of myself coming into being out of, yet somehow in response to, that radiant darkness. My whole consciousness of myself and everything else has changed. I feel as if the back of my head has been sawn off so that it is no longer the 60-year-old John who looks out at the world, but the shining dark infinite void that in some extraordinary way is also "I."

And what I perceive with my eyes and other senses is a whole world that seems to be coming fresh-minted into existence *moment by moment*, each instant evoking the utter delight of "Behold, it is very good." Here yet again I am constantly up against paradox when I try to describe the experience. Thus, in one sense, I feel as if I am infinitely far back in sensing the world, yet at the same time I feel the very opposite, as if my consciousness is no longer inside my head at all, but out there in the things I am experiencing . . .

JOHN WREN-LEWIS

Liberation in All Places

Don't seek a Buddha, don't seek a teaching, don't seek a community. Don't seek virtue, knowledge, intellectual understanding, and so on. When feelings of defilement and purity are ended, still don't hold to this non-seeking and consider it right. Don't dwell at the point of ending, and don't long for heavens or fear hells. When you are unhindered by bondage or freedom, then this is called liberation of mind and body in all places.

A Buddha is one who does not seek. In seeking this, you turn away from it. The principle is the principle of non-seeking, when you seek it, you lose it. If you cling to non-seeking, this is the same as seeking. If you cling to non-striving, this is the same as striving.

PAI-CHANG

It is just as easy to cling to concepts about "living in the now" or non-seeking. Lay them all down, even the beautiful ones you are reading in this book.

When I returned to my teacher Ajahn Chah after completing a long period of intensive training in other monasteries, I told him about the insights and special experiences I had encountered. He listened kindly and then responded, "It's just something else to let go of, isn't it?"

We need to remember that where we are going is here, that any practice is simply a means to open our heart to what is in front of us. Where we already are is the path and the goal.

JACK KORNFIELD

In seeking, we accumulate mountains of baggage that obscure the simple truth. Set it all down. Every day. Every minute.

Because It's There

The real meaning of praying without ceasing, it seems to me, is that the divine presence or eternal values in the present moment begin to become more transparent; they became a kind of fourth dimension of the three-dimensional world. The awareness of God's presence at the subtlest level of all realities begins to be a kind of spontaneous addition to ordinary awareness, not through a thought or through any effort of ours at the time, but simply because it's there, and our capacity to perceive it has awakened through progress in contemplative prayer. Accessing the divine presence within ourselves seems to unlock the capacity to perceive it in all events, however opaque they may seem to ordinary human perceptions. So to pray without ceasing is to be aware of the divine presence all the time as a spontaneous part of all reality.

FR. THOMAS KEATING

Transforming Dragons

If only we arrange our life in accordance with the principle which tells us that we must always trust in the difficult, then what now appears to us as the most alien will become our most intimate and trusted experience. How could we forget those ancient myths that stand at the beginning of all races, the myths about dragons that at the last moment are transformed into princesses? Perhaps all the dragons in our lives are princesses who are only waiting to see us act, just once, with beauty and courage. Perhaps everything that frightens us is, in its deepest essence, something helpless that wants our love.

So you mustn't be frightened . . . if a sadness rises in front of you, larger than any you have ever seen; if an anxiety, like light and cloud-shadows, moves over your hands and over everything you do. You must realize that something is happening to you, that life has not forgotten you, that it holds you in its hand and will not let you fall. Why do you want to shut out of your life any uneasiness, any misery, any depression, since after all you don't know what work these conditions are doing inside of you?

RAINER MARIA RILKE

What are you shutting out of your life? Take this moment to welcome whatever it is back in from the cold.

Be
Melting
Snow

Lo, I am with you always means that when you look for God,

God is in the look of your eyes,

in the thought of looking, nearer to you than your self,

or things that have happened to you

There's no need to go outside.

Be melting snow.
Wash yourself of yourself.

A white flower grows in the quietness.
Let your tongue become that flower.

RUMI

It is all one taste.

Only in the Present

There is neither past nor future; there is only the present. Yesterday was the present when you experienced it; tomorrow will also be the present when you experience it. Therefore, experience takes place only in the present, and beyond and apart from experience, nothing exists. Even the present is mere imagination, for the sense of time is purely mental.

Because people want something elaborate and mysterious, so many religions have come into existence. Only those who are mature can understand the matter in its naked simplicity.

Because people love mystery and not the truth, religions cater to them, eventually bringing them around to the Self. Whatever be the means adopted, you must at least return to the Self; so why not abide in the Self here and now?

RAMANA MAHARSHI

Why suffer a grueling journey that will only ever return you to this moment?

Today I Was Happy, So I Made This Poem

As the plump squirrel scampers
Across the roof of the corncrib,
The moon suddenly stands up in the darkness,
And I see that it is impossible to die.
Each moment of time is a mountain.
An eagle rejoices in the oak trees of heaven,
Crying
This is what I wanted.

JAMES WRIGHT

Can you honestly say, "This is what I want"?

Dive
Deeply

Nowhere does [the Buddha] promise a freedom divorced from the grist of our everyday lives. Nowhere does he speak of a disembodied, transcendent experience or realm. The Buddha encourages us to remove the dust from our eyes. Awakening is here and now, in the stones of the rivers, in the sunbeams on the grass, in this very body, mind, and life. Nowhere is there the encouragement to annihilate life, but simply to let go of our illusions. In being both a mystic and not a mystic, the Buddha ended the long schism between the sacred and the mundane, and the tension of being pulled in opposing directions. We are not invited to transcend the world but to dive deeply into it and find wisdom. We are asked to be in the world, but not of it—to cling to nothing, to reject nothing. Awakening invites our acknowledgment that we are social, sexual, spiritual embodied beings. Embracing our wholeness, we are alert to the doors of awakening offered to us throughout our life. We are Buddhas with amnesia, learning to remember ourselves.

CHRISTINA FELDMAN

Being Here

The real human problem has to do with how things are right **Here**, right **Now**. **This** is where we find life and death. It's not life now and death later. **This** is where it *all* happens. We don't die in the future; we die **Now**, in the present moment. And so, whatever it is, we must deal with it **Here**. We cannot set it off at a distance and objectify it. We can't deal with anything if we push it off to some other place or some other time. The Truth is that we can't go off somewhere else. There's no such place, for Reality is forever immediately at hand.

The World simply does not function the way we imagine. All we need to verify that it doesn't is to **just see**. Being **Here** is just **this**. Nothing ever comes and goes. We're still in the boundless room where we merely rearrange things and thoughts out of blind habit and ignorance. We just move the furniture in a desperate attempt to get things just right, so that we may satisfy ourselves. Yet all the while, we never seek to inquire about the nature of the room itself. **This** room, where you truly are, has no doors or windows. You'll never leave **Here**. In fact, you'll never arrive either. You're already **Here**. You can *only* be **Here**. It's because we can't leave the room, we can't leave **Here** and **Now**, that we should study what **this immediacy** is . . .

STEVE HAGEN

Imagine that the room you are in right now is your entire life. This is IT! There is nowhere else to go. No exits, no escape routes. Prison or palace? It's up to you.

Do not discriminate,
do not reflect,
do not alter,
but let the mind be relaxed,
For the unmodulated mind is the natural treasure of
the unborn,
The nondual path of wisdom-gone-beyond.[29]

NAGARJUNA

Ultimately you are not taking responsibility for life until you take responsibility for this moment—Now. This is because Now is the only place where life can be found.

ECKHART TOLLE

No longer forward nor behind
I look in hope or fear;
But, grateful, take the good I find
The best of now and here

JOSH GREENLEAF WHITTIER

---

[29]"Wisdom Gone Beyond"—*Prajnaparamita* in Sanskrit, meaning the ultimate reality, transcendent wisdom.

Simply Noticing

Sit down in a comfortable position that enables you to keep your back straight. Relax your abdomen, drop your shoulders. Let your eyes rest 3 or 4 feet in front of you. Take a few deep breaths and then let your breathing return to normal. Feel your body breathing. Feel the air enter your body, fill your body, and leave your body.

Thoughts will arise and pass away. Feelings will arise and pass away. You may hear sounds, smell odors, see sights, feel sensations. Just notice them, resisting nothing, holding onto nothing (resisting no thing, holding onto no thing), allowing everything to be as it is.

Just sit—not trying to accomplish anything, not trying to change anything, especially yourself. Breathe in and breathe out.

Aware	Right here
Alert	Right now
Attentive	Accepting what is
Present	Simply noticing

CHERI HUBER

Hidden
Dimensions

The key to this freedom is understanding that *in the present moment, there is no time.* The gospels of the world's great religions make reference to the "eternal present" in their teaching, instructing seekers after God to look no farther than where they're standing for the kingdom of heaven. In other words, *eternity is now,* and by learning to "lose track of time" through present focus, we begin to discover hidden dimensions to everyday experience, which have always been there for us, but have been veiled by our being time-bound. The moment is a doorway into eternity.

RAM DASS

Come to Your Senses

For enlightenment to happen, the perceiver must turn right around and wake up to the fact that he is face to face with his own nature—that HE IS IT. The spiritual seeker ultimately finds that he was already at the destination, that he himself IS what he had been seeking and he was in fact already home.

RAMESH S. BALSEKAR

Come to your senses. It is not the things of this world, be they chocolate or brown rice, that lead you astray. Losing your way comes from giving no mind to what is present while chasing after imaginary pleasures which are illusions and unobtainable. To wake up is to know what is already yours.

EDWARD ESPE BROWN

Y ou are not ready to accept the fact that you
have to give up. A complete and total "surrender" . . . It is a state of hopelessness which
says that there is no way out. . . . Any movement in
any direction, on any dimension, at any level, is taking you away
from Yourself. . . .

U. G. KRISHNAMURTI

I think it's a mistake to ever look for hope outside of one's self.
One day the house smells of fresh bread, the next of smoke and
blood. One day you faint because the gardener cuts his finger
off, within a week you're climbing over corpses of children
bombed in a subway. What hope can there be if that is so? I tried
to die near the end of the war. The same dream returned each
night until I dared not go to sleep and grew quite ill. I dreamed
I had a child, and even in the dream I saw it was my life, and it
was an idiot, and I ran away. But it always crept onto my lap
again, clutched at my clothes. Until I thought, if I could kiss it,
whatever in it was my own, perhaps I could sleep. And I bent to
its broken face, and it was horrible . . . but I kissed it. I think one
must finally take one's life in one's arms.

ARTHUR MILLER

Appreciating Sacredness

The way to experience nowness is to realize that this very moment, this very point in your life, is always *the* occasion. So the consideration of where you are and what you are, on the spot, is very important. That is one reason that your family situation, your domestic everyday life, is so important. You should regard your home as sacred, as a golden opportunity to experience nowness. Appreciating sacredness begins very simply by taking an interest in all the details of your life. Interest is simply applying awareness to what goes on in your everyday life—awareness while you're cooking, awareness while you're driving, awareness while you're changing diapers, even awareness while you're arguing. Such awareness can help to free you from speed, chaos, neurosis, and resentment of all kinds. It can free you from the obstacles to nowness, so that you can cheer up on the spot, all the time.

CHOGYAM TRUNGPA

Renunciation

You have absolutely nothing to give up
Nothing to surrender, nothing to let go of.
You are already liberated.
How can you believe that you have to let go of
something
That never existed?
You believe that you have to let go of your attachments.
How can the Self have attachments?
You think you have to surrender all of your fears,
All of your depressions,
All of the things that have been bothering you.
Surrender to whom? Those things are not yours.
They do not belong to you.

You are pure Reality. You are the Imperishable Self.
Never were you born, never did you prevail,
And never will you leave.
You are the One. The All-Pervading One.
Consequently, you have absolutely nothing to give up.
For you had never anything to begin with.

ROBERT ADAMS

It is not about letting go of anything. It is about
letting everything be.

God Is Always Now

The state of completeness is always present. It is never future or past. God is always now.

Our meditation is always . . . another step into the eternal now of God. Every time we meditate, we take another step into the divine life that enlivens, brings to fullness, everyone who opens herself to it by taking this step of turning from self. The paradox we discover in the course of taking this step day by day arises from the divine paradox—a life which is wholly present, wholly without reveries or daydreams, where everything is actualized and complete, and yet which is always expanding into transcendence. The divine paradox is love. [B]ut like all growth, this entry into the divinizing experience of the present moment involves pain. It is the pain of all maturing. It arises from the need to leave behind us every earlier state of development, all that we have been, in favor of what we are summoned to become.

JOHN MAIN

Thank
U
(excerpt)

thank you India
thank you terror
thank you disillusionment
thank you frailty
thank you consequence
thank you thank you silence
how 'bout me not blaming you for everything
how 'bout me enjoying the moment for once
how 'bout how good it feels to finally forgive you
how 'bout grieving it all one at a time
the moment I let go of it was the moment
I got more than I could handle
the moment I jumped off of it
was the moment I touched down
how 'bout no longer being masochistic
how 'bout remembering your divinity
how 'bout unabashedly bawling your eyes out
how 'bout not equating death with stopping
thank you India
thank you providence
thank you disillusionment
thank you nothingness
thank you clarity
thank you thank you silence

ALANIS MORISSETTE

Imagine gratitude for feeling terrified; all-encompassing, joyfully embraces what is.

315

Simply
Allow

We need to train in this thought-free wakefulness, but not by meditating on it or imagining it. It is primordially present already. Yet this present wakefulness gets caught up in thinking. To get free of thought, simply recognize; recognize your present wakefulness. Don't forget; don't get distracted. That doesn't mean to sit and force oneself to be undistracted and unforgetting. Trying like that only fouls it up. Simply allow your basic state to be undistracted nonmeditation. When all the activities of dualistic mind dissolve, when we are utterly stable in the unconfined empty cognizance, there is no longer any basis for remaining in the three realms of samsara.

TULKU URGYEN RINPOCHE

Dzogchen masters like Tulken Urgyen point out how to recognize this natural wakefulness without effort or forced attention. This relaxed sense of allowing is such a relief.

Your Own Mind

Q: From all you have just said, Mind is the Buddha; but it is not clear as to what sort of mind is meant by this "Mind which is the Buddha."

A: How many minds have you got?

Q: But is the Buddha the ordinary mind or the Enlightened mind?

A: Where on earth do you keep your "ordinary mind" and your "Enlightened mind"? . . . In the teaching . . . it is clearly explained that the ordinary and Enlightened minds are illusions. You don't understand. All this clinging to the idea of things existing is to mistake vacuity for the truth. How can such conceptions not be illusory? Being illusory, they hide Mind from you. If you would only rid yourself of the concepts of ordinary and Enlightened, you would find that there is no other Buddha than the Buddha in your own Mind.

Q: Just now you said that the beginningless past and the present are the same. What do you mean by that?

A: It is just because of your SEEKING that you make a difference between them. If you were to stop seeking, how could there be any difference between them?

HUANG PO

317

Today in My Eyes

[When he was growing up in Alabama, Truman's companions were his dog Queenie and an elderly cousin whom he refers to as "my friend." His cousin said this just before she died.]

"My, how foolish I am!" my friend cries, suddenly alert, like a woman remembering too late she has biscuits in the oven. "You know what I've always thought?" she asks in a tone of discovery, and not smiling at me but a point beyond. "I've always thought a body would have to be sick and dying before they saw the Lord. And I imagined that when He came it would be like looking at the Baptist window: pretty as colored glass with the sun pouring through, such a shine you don't know it's getting dark. And it's been a comfort to think of that shine taking away all the spooky feeling. But I'll wager it never happens. I'll wager at the very end a body realizes the Lord has already shown Himself. That things as they are"—her hand circles in a gesture that gathers clouds and kites and grass and Queenie pawing earth over her bone—"just what they've always seen, was seeing Him. As for me, I could leave the world with today in my eyes."

TRUMAN CAPOTE

Face to face, all the time.

The Whole Point

I saw everything, just as it is now, is IT—is the whole point of there being life and a universe. I saw what when the *Upanishads* said, "That thou art!" or "All this world is Brahman," they meant just exactly what they said. Each thing, each event, each experience in its inescapable nowness and in all its own particular individuality was precisely what it should be, and so much so that it acquired a divine authority and originality. It struck me with the fullest clarity that none of this depended on my seeing it to be so; that was the way things were, whether I understood it or not, and if I did not understand, that was IT too. Furthermore, I felt that I now understood what Christianity might mean by the love of God—namely, that despite the commonsensical imperfection of things, they were nonetheless loved by God just as they are, and that this loving of them was at the same time the godding of them.

ALAN WATTS

Nothing but God

Now what, monks, is the All? It is just the eye and the visible objects, the ear and sounds, the nose and odors, the tongue and taste, the body and tangible objects of the mind. This, monks, is called the All.

THE BUDDHA

As I sat quietly in the little chapel, I became aware that the massive solidity of those huge stone pillars was an illusion. Like my own body and that of my friend they were no more than pulsating columns of totally insubstantial atoms of power. It seemed that they were vibrating with a ceaseless manifestation of power—rather as a chord of music will vibrate in the air long after the player has ceased. Their solidity was total illusion. The whole universe was an illusion. There is nothing but pure Energy—nothing but God.

RERU ACCOUNT

Now, when you are introduced [to your own intrinsic awareness], the method for entering into it involves three considerations:

Thoughts in the past are clear and empty and leave no traces behind.

Thoughts in the future are fresh and unconditioned by anything.

And in the present moment, when [your mind] remains in its own condition without constructing anything, awareness at that moment in itself is quite ordinary.

And when you look into yourself in this way nakedly (without any discursive thoughts), since there is only pure observing, there will be found a lucid clarity without anyone being there who is the observer; Only a naked manifest awareness is present. [This awareness] is empty and immaculately pure, not being created by anything whatsoever. It is authentic and unadulterated, without any duality of clarity and emptiness.

PADMASAMBHAVA

Just Let False Views Cease

It's no use to seek truth,
Just let false views cease.
Don't abide in duality
And take care not to seek,
For as soon as there is yes and no,
The mind is lost in confusion.
Two comes forth from one,
But don't hold even the one,
For when even the one mind is unborn,
The myriad things are flawless
Without flaws, without things.

SENG TS'AN

How do we sort out the true from the false?
With moment-to-moment self-inquiry. No seeking; just seeing.

Just a cup of tea. Just another opportunity for healing. Just the hand reaching out to receive the handle of the cup. Just noticing hot. Noticing texture and fragrance. Just a cup of tea. Just this moment in newness. Just the hand touching the cup. Just the arm retracting. The fragrance increasing as the cup nears the lips. So present. Noticing the bottom lip receiving heat from the cup, the top lip arched to receive the fluid within. Noticing the first taste of tea before the tea even touches the lips. The fragrance and the heat rising into the mouth. The first noticing of flavor. The touch of warm tea on willing tongue. The tongue moving the tea about in the mouth. The intention to swallow. The warmth that extends down into the stomach. What a wonderful cup of tea. The tea of peace, of satisfaction. Drinking a cup of tea, I stop the war.

STEPHEN LEVINE

Present at Every Breath

The technique I use is called "alertness meditation," which is simply a sense of being present at every breath and understanding that the breath is the opening and closing of the door to life. It's just sitting in as close to a lotus posture as my battered body can manage and being conscious of my breath coming and going. Of course, the mind will race in to fill the gaps, but every breath brings me back to an inner silence and inner stillness. Eventually, there comes a sense of connectedness, a realization that everything that is exists in the same moment. This is now. This is now. This is now. And so on. The common existence in this same nowness is what connects everything, so that even the smallest microcosm in our particular world is connected to the most distant part of the universe.

PHIL JACKSON

So who are you? You are not objects out there, you are not feelings, you are not thoughts—you are effortlessly aware of all those, so you are not those. Who or what are you? Say it this way to yourself: I *have* feelings, but I am not those feelings. Who am I? I *have* thoughts, but I am not those thoughts. Who am I? . . .

So you push back into the source of your own awareness. You push back into the Witness, and you rest in the Witness. I am not objects, not feelings, not desires, not thoughts. But then people usually make a big mistake. They think that if they rest in the Witness, they are going to see something or feel something— something really neat and special. But you won't see anything. If you see something, that is just another object—another feeling, another thought, another sensation, another image. But those are all objects, those are what you are *not*.

No, as you rest in the Witness—all you will notice is a sense of freedom, a sense of liberation, a sense of release—release from the terrible constriction of identifying with these puny little finite objects, your little body and little mind and little ego, all of which are objects that can be seen, and thus are not the true Seer, the real Self, the pure Witness, which is what you really are.

KEN WILBER

So, who are you?

Inexpressible Radiance

When I look at the true nature of the universe,
All is the never-failing expression
Of the mysterious reality.
Every particle of matter
In each and every moment
In all places
Is nothing other than the inexpressible radiance
Of the Tathagata.[30]

TOREI ZENJI

---

[30]Another term for the Buddha.

Listen to the Stones

Be still
Listen to the stones of the wall.
Be silent, they try
To speak your

Name.
Listen
To the living walls.

Who are you?
Who
Are you? Whose
Silence are you?

THOMAS MERTON

Today
Is
Your
Lucky
Day

Do not look back. And do not dream about the future, either. It will neither give you back the past, nor satisfy your other daydreams. Your duty, your reward—your destiny—are here and now.

DAG HAMMARSKJÖLD

Forget mistakes. Forget failures. Forget everything except what you're going to do now and do it. Today is your lucky day.

WILL DURANT

Happiness not in another place, but this place . . . not for another hour, but this hour . . .

WALT WHITMAN

As It Actually Looked

It happened on a May morning—I have forgotten the year—but I can still point to the exact spot where it occurred, on a forest path on Martinsberg above Baden, Switzerland. As I strolled through the freshly greened woods filled with bird song and lit up by the morning sun, all at once everything appeared in an uncommonly clear light. Was this something I had simply failed to notice before? Was I suddenly discovering the spring forest as it actually looked? It shone with the most beautiful radiance, speaking to the heart, as though it wanted to encompass me in its majesty. I was filled with an indescribable sensation of joy, oneness, and blissful security.

. . . While still a child, I experienced several more of these deeply euphoric moments on my rambles through forest and meadow. It was these experiences that shaped the main outlines of my world view and convinced me of the existence of a miraculous, powerful, unfathomable reality that was hidden from everyday sight.

DR. ALBERT HOFFMAN

Eternity

Eternity is not something that begins after you are dead. It is going on all the time.

CHARLOTTE PERKINS GILMAN

If we take eternity to mean not infinite temporal duration, but timelessness, eternal life is theirs who live in the present.

LUDWIG WITTGENSTEIN

At dawn Henry picked up his stick.
It wasn't too short or too long.
It wasn't too thick or too thin.
Like the wilderness, it was the way it should be.
Henry looked out over the world.
And then descended into the rising mist.

THOMAS LOCKER

Beyond Wishing and Dreaming

It is only when we get beyond fantasy, beyond wishing and dreaming, that the real conversion takes place and we awake re-born, the dream re-becomes reality. For reality is the goal, deny it how we will. And we can approach it only by an ever-expanding consciousness, by burning more and more brightly, until even memory itself vanishes.

When the individual is wholly creative, one with destiny, there is neither time nor space, nor birth and death. The god-feeling becomes so intense that everything, organic and inorganic, beats with divine rhythm. At the moment of supreme individuation, when the identity of all things is sensed and one is at the same time utterly and blissfully alone, the umbilical cord is at last cut. There is neither a longing for the womb nor a longing for the beyond. The sure feeling of eternality. Beyond this there is no evolution, only a perpetual movement from creation to creation.

HENRY MILLER

One
Is the
Transformation

So the eternity we seek has always been "with" us—closer to us than we are to ourselves, to paraphrase Augustine, for all that we need to do is to "forget" ourselves and realize that we have always been. But because of the habitual restlessness of our minds, we are now not able to experience the present—to *be* present—and so we overlook something about it. What would such a nondual experience of time be like? Not the static "block universe" . . . for my point here is that *the immutability of the Now is not incompatible with change.* There would still be transformation, although experienced differently since one *is* the transformation rather than an observer *of* it. Such change would be a smoother, more continuous flux than we are familiar with, since without anxious thought-construction and thought-projection, the mind would not be jumping, staccato-fashion, from one perch to another in order to fixate itself. In one way, nothing would be different: "I" would still rise in the morning, eat breakfast, go to work, and so on. But at the same time there would also be something completely timeless about these activities . . . In place of the apparent solid I that *does* them, there would be an empty and immutable serene quality to them.

DAVID LOY

The truth is everywhere, in all of our experiences. We do not have to fitfully try to have a sublime, magical experience and, in this effort, disdain what is actually happening. We do not have to struggle to find the truth. Every single moment is expressive of the truth of our lives, when we know how to look.

SHARON SALZBERG

Don't move. Just die over and over. Don't anticipate. Nothing can save you now because you have only this moment. Not even enlightenment will help you now because there are no other moments. With no future, be true to yourself and express yourself fully. Don't move.

SHUNRYU SUZUKI

The Answer (excerpt)

A light went on inside my brain:
"Aha!" I cried with glee.
The world was bright and boisterous,
And I—released, rejoisterous—
Felt rounder than a pea.

And ever since that bulgy night
Inside the whiffle bog,
I've lived my days in clarity,
My evenings in hilarity,
As fragrant as a frog.

STEPHEN MITCHELL

Your Buddhas

People who enlighten me are all my Buddhas. Instead of trying to find Buddhas in high and precious places, shouldn't you be able to find your Buddhas in your town, in your marketplaces, and in your streets? Everyone has valuable and enlightening qualities. If you learned and practiced those qualities, it would be like meeting the Buddha and practicing his teachings.

JAE WOONG KIM

When
Death
Comes
(excerpt)

And therefore I look upon everything
as a brotherhood and a sisterhood,
and I look upon time as no more than an idea,
and I consider eternity as another possibility,

and I think of each life as a flower, as common
as a field daisy, and as singular,

and each name a comfortable music in the mouth,
tending, as all music does, toward silence,

and each body a lion of courage, and something
precious to the earth.

When it's over, I want to say: all my life
I was a bride married to amazement.
I was the bridegroom, taking the world into my arms.

MARY OLIVER

336

This Stubborn Illusion

On the fifteenth of March 1955, Albert Einstein wrote a note of condolence to the family of his friend Michele Besso, who had died a week earlier. The letter begins with an excruciating confession about his own life. "What I admired most about Michele was the fact that he was able to live so many years with one woman, not only in peace but in constant unity, something I have lamentably failed at twice." Further on, after recalling his meeting with Michele almost six decades earlier when they were university students in Zurich, and the difficulty in keeping in touch through the intervening years, Einstein rouses himself from his melancholy and soars to a higher plane. His concluding passage rings with pure spiritual power. "So, in quitting this strange world he has once again preceded me by a little. That doesn't mean anything. For those of us who believe in physics, this separation between past, present and future is only an illusion, albeit a stubborn one." Less than four weeks later Einstein followed his life-long friend out of this strange world.

HANS CHRISTIAN VON BAEYER

Einstein said that the experience of the Now is something special for Man, something essentially different from the past and the future, and that this important difference does not and cannot occur within science.

337

Music of Silence

Monasticism's central message, expressed through the chant, is the supreme importance of time and how we relate to it: how we caretake and *respond* to the present moment, to what is before us now.

The message of the hours is to live daily with the *real* rhythms of the day. To live responsively, consciously, and intentionally directing our lives from within, not being swept along by the demands of the clock, by external agendas, by mere reactions to whatever happens. By living in the real rhythms, we ourselves become more real. We learn to listen to the music of the moment, to hear its sweet implorings, its sober directives. We learn to dance a little in our hearts, to open our inner gates a crack more, to hearken to the music of silence, the divine life breath of the universe.

DAVID STEINDL-RAST AND SHARON LEBELL

Direct
Contact

When sufficient mindfulness and equanimity are brought to bear on ordinary experience, we arrive at purification and insight. And, as a result of the purification and insight, our intrinsic happiness, our true birthright and spiritual reality, gets uncovered and we discover that what we thought was the world of phenomena—the world of time, space, and matter—turns out to really be a world of spiritual energy, and that we are in direct contact with it moment by moment. Because, when the senses become purified, when the inner conflicts—at all levels—have been broken up, the flow of these ordinary senses turns into a prayer, a mantra, a sacred song, and we find that, just by living our life, we are in moment by moment contact with the Source.

SHINZEN YOUNG

Falling
Awake

One night as I was falling asleep my mind suddenly stopped its ceaseless activity and became still. It was as if it had turned inward and collapsed onto itself. I felt a soft effusion of supreme comfortableness engulf my being and my mind was for a moment unbounded with no thoughts or perceptions. I was filled with a profound feeling of well being and happiness. I felt wrapped in a blanket of love and safety, or rather I was That, the wrapper and the wrapped all at once. There was no differentiation of experience. I WAS that state, nothing else. It was not me experiencing something outside of me. It was not happiness about any particular thing, but an unconditional, all pervading bliss that depends on nothing outside of itself. It was as if the river of ever-active consciousness moving in streams of thoughts and perceptions had arrived at the ocean of silent, ever full, unbounded awareness.

I had no idea what it was, no frame of reference to explain it, and it didn't even occur to me to try to talk to someone about it. Many nights I would "try" to make it happen again, try to capture it, but trying only seemed to push it away. I was about eight or nine years old at the time.

DAVID W. ORME-JOHNSON

Experiences come and they go, but awareness is always here.

"No, not in a future eternal life, but in eternal life here. There are moments, you reach moments, and time suddenly stands still, and it will become eternal."

"You hope to reach such a moment?"

"Yes."

"That'll scarcely be possible in our time," Nikolay responded slowly and, as it were, dreamily; the two spoke without the slightest irony. "In the Apocalypse the angel swears that there will be no more time."

"I know. That's very true; distinct and exact. When all mankind attains happiness then there will be no more time, for there'll be no need of it, a very true thought."

"Where will they put it?"

"Nowhere. Time's not an object but an idea. It will be extinguished in the mind."

FYODOR DOSTOYEVSKY

Who I Am

I have spied that secret place from time to time, usually as through a glass darkly, but now and again with blazing clarity. One time it glowed from a red carnation, incandescent in a florist's window. Once it shimmered in drifting pollen, once in a sky needled with ice. I have seen it wound in a scarf of dust around a whirling pony. I have seen it glinting from a pebble on the slate bed of a creek. I have slipped into the secret place while watching hawks, while staring down the throat of a lily, while brushing my wife's hair. Metaphors are inexact. The experience is not a glimpsing of realms beyond, nor of becoming someone new, but of acknowledging, briefly and utterly, who I am.

SCOTT RUSSELL SANDERS

When we drop the idea of "special," all things are seen as naturally radiant and extraordinary.

Gratefully Be

The whole experience was one of joy and gratitude which mounted at times to ecstasy and deepened at others into a vast, profound, illuminated peace. There was no negative emotion, no doubt, terror or struggle—only complete trust in life and the mystery sustaining life. It was immortality *now;* eternity palpably *present.* One wanted to go nowhere, change nothing, just gratefully *be.* The only urgency was that everyone else should realize the same beatitude, because it belongs to everyone by gift of whatever ineffable mystery is responsible for it. Not that pain and sorrow do not exist. They do, but on a more superficial, impermanent level—perhaps one could say on the training and testing level.

As the sensation came on after about twenty minutes of intercessory prayer, it gradually increased in intensity to a great glowing joy. I found myself drenched in gratitude for life . . . I was overcome by excess of life. I could hardly bear it. I felt I might die of it, although I knew that to be impossible.

RERU ACCOUNT

Having a Quiet Mind

You say tranquility of the mind and a peaceful heart are essential. Is that so? Or, is that merely a theory, merely a desire? Because we are so disturbed, distracted, we want that quietness, that tranquility—which then is merely an escape. It is not a necessity; it is an escape. When we see the necessity of it, when we are convinced it is the only thing that matters, the only thing that is essential—then, do we ask the method for it? Is a method necessary when you see something is essential?

Method involves time, does it not? If not now, then eventually—tomorrow, in a couple of years—I shall be tranquil. Which means, you do not see the necessity of being tranquil. And so, the "how" becomes a distraction; the method becomes a way of postponing the essentiality of tranquility. And that is why you have all these meditations, these phony, false controls, to get eventual tranquility of the mind, and the various methods of how to discipline in order to acquire that tranquility. Which means, you do not see the necessity, the immediate necessity, of having a still mind. When you see the necessity of it, then there is no inquiry into the method at all. Then you see the importance of having a quiet mind, and you **have** a quiet mind.

J. KRISHNAMURTI

344

A visiting monk asked: "In your sermon the other evening, you stated that everyone innately possesses the Buddha Mind. While I'm grateful for your instruction, it seems to me that if everyone were endowed with the Buddha Mind, deluded thoughts couldn't arise."

The Master replied, "Right now, as you're saying this, what delusions *are* there?"

BANKEI

You
See
Through

One instant is eternity;
eternity is in the now;
When you see through this one instant,
you see through the one who sees.

WU-MEN

The Task

When each day
is sacred

when each hour
is sacred

when each instant
is sacred

earth and you
space and you
bearing the sacred
through time

you'll reach
the fields of light.

GUILLEVIC

And these are the fields of light.

Asking the Way

You blockheads who ask what Buddha is

should start asking about every sentient being instead.

Ask about everything.

When you're hungry

ask about food.

Ask the moonlight about the way.

Find a port where lemon trees bloom

where lemon trees bloom.

Ask about places to drink in the port.

Ask and ask till nothing's left to ask.

KO UN

What a beautiful lemon tree! Take a chance and ask what you're afraid to ask.

Dry up the remains of your past and have nothing for your future. If you do not cling to the present then you can go from place to place in peace.

THE BUDDHA

Pure awareness of nowness is the real buddha.

DUDJOM RINPOCHE

Don't prolong the past,
Don't invite the future,
Don't alter your innate wakefulness,
Don't fear appearances.
There is nothing more than that!

PATRUL RINPOCHE

When we discuss the real present, it can only be *ripga* (intrinsic awareness), the spaciousness of *rigpa*, not a projection of thought that labels something "the present moment." The label "the present moment" can never be the present; it is already out of date. . . . It is therefore impossible to nail down "the present" aside from it being your own invented label. It cannot be found; it does not exist. The only real nowness is therefore emptiness. There is no other possibility.

TSOKNYI RINPOCHE

Full Possession

Life is not meant to be rich in spiritual significance at some distant date, but it can be so at every moment if the mind is disburdened of illusions. Only through a clear and tranquil mind is the true nature of spiritual infinity grasped—not as something that is yet to be but that already has been, is, and ever will be eternal Self-fulfillment. When every moment is rich with eternal significance, there is neither the lingering clinging to the dead past nor a longing expectation for the future but an integral living in the eternal Now. Only through such living can the spiritual infinity of the Truth be realized in life.

It is not right to deprive the present of all importance by subordinating it to an end in the future. For this means the imaginary accumulation of all importance in the imagined future rather than the perception and realization of the true importance of everything that exists in the eternal Now. There cannot be an ebb and flow in eternity, no meaningless intervals between intermittent harvests, but a fullness of being that cannot suffer impoverishment for a single instant. When life seems to be idle or empty, it is not due to any curtailment of the infinity of the Truth but to one's own lack of capacity to enter into its full possession . . .

MEHER BABA

Like a Homecoming

I lie on the seashore, the sparkling flood blue-shimmering in my dreamy eyes; light breezes flutter in the distance; the thud of the waves, charging and breaking over in foam, beats thrillingly and drowsily upon the shore—or upon the ear? I cannot tell. The far and the near become blurred into one; outside and inside merge into one another. Nearer and nearer, friendlier, like a homecoming, sounds the thud of the waves; now, like a thundering pulse, they beat in my head, now they beat over my soul, wrapping it round, consuming it, while at the same time my soul floats out of me as a blue waste of waters. Outside and inside are one. The whole symphony of sensations fades away into one tone, all senses become one sense, which is one with feeling; the world expires in the soul and the soul dissolves in the world.

KARL JOEL

Who Is Here Now?

Q: Should I wait for the direct experience to occur?

A: No! Waiting means that it is not already here. Waiting for it is putting it to a future date and not having it Now. What is not Here Now will never be your own fundamental nature!

I do not tell you to wait for the future. Just tell me who you are right now. If you are not already what you are, you become something else and if you become something else you will have to be lost. Therefore don't hanker after things which are not already Here. So find out, who is here now! Not in the past or the future. What is present Here Now?

H. W. L. POONJA (POONJAJI)

Here is another useful question. Whenever you say "I . . . ," ask yourself, "Who is here now?"

352

Overlooking Our Greatest Gift

We search everywhere outside ourselves to try to find ourselves. We collect experiences, relationships, knowledge, and objects. We hope for recognition from others to validate our importance. But while we may have found pleasure or rewards in various ways, we have often overlooked our greatest gift, hidden in plain sight—our own passionate presence. We overlook this gift because we are so busy searching elsewhere for something more. As long as we depend on an enhanced sense of ourselves to be happy, we are likely to be disappointed. Telling ourselves stories about what is missing forces us into a relentless pursuit of desires, akin, as my teacher Poonjaji would say, to beasts of burden driven by a madman. Happiness comes in relaxed simplicity, living in present awareness, and contentment with this life that is granted.

What is known as realization is merely feeling this immaculate presence here and now, realizing or being fully cognizant of the ordinary miracle of just being. This needs no attainment since it is already occurring. It requires no special circumstances, no life epiphanies, no meritorious preparations. It is fully present, each moment of our lives. It stays ever fresh and innocent despite our sorrows, regrets, and whatever damage or failures we feel we have sustained. No suffering or transgressions have marred it, just as no exalted deeds have enhanced it. Countless thoughts and experiences have come and gone, and none of them have adhered.

CATHERINE INGRAM

The Seeker Is Reality Itself

Don't hold your mind "here," don't seek "there" after objects. Remain without artifice exactly on the mind of the looker and thinker. Don't hold your mind "here," don't seek "there" for the object of meditation. Remain without artifice exactly on the mind that is doing the meditation.

Your mind is not found by seeking. Mind itself has been empty from the very beginning. Seeking is not necessary, for the seeker is reality itself. Remain unwaveringly on the one who is seeking. Understanding or not-understanding, true or not true, existing or not-existing—no matter what comes, just remain without artifice on the one who is thinking. Good or bad, pleasing or dirty, happy or sad, for whatever recollection arises, without accepting or rejecting, just remain without artifice on the one who is doing the recollecting. Desirable or undesirable, for whatever arises, just remain without artifice on the arising.

PATRUL RINPOCHE[31]

[31]From *Simply Being,* translated by James Low.

Passing Backwards

L et's be clear: the awakening does in no way constitute an end. One can only attain it by passing backwards through all intentions, all motivations—including that of attaining the awakening. One must strip oneself of all one's intentions, all one's wishes, even the highest. One doesn't move towards the awakening, for if one can invoke even the slightest argument for moving towards awakening, one turns his back to it. In fact, the infinite value, once again, offers nothing.

STEPHEN JOURDAIN

Don't Turn Your Head Away

To hold on to the self is corrupt, to not hold on to the self is pure. It is just like a mad dog who is always trying to get more and more to eat. Where is the Buddha to be found? Thousands and ten thousands of people are "seeking-for-Buddha" fools.

When the world was not, there was still this reality. When the world is destroyed, this reality is not destroyed. Take one look at me, I am nothing other than I am. The True Self is simply this. Right here what more is there to be sought for? At such a time, don't turn your head away or change your expression. If you do so, it is immediately lost.

JOSHU

Take a look at how beautiful you are right now. What use is there in trying to be holy or enlightened?

I will now point directly to the original mind in you, to enable you to awaken, you clear your mind to listen to what I say . . . I will point out one entry way, by which you can return to the source.

Do you hear the cawing of the crows and the chattering of the jays? *Student:* I hear them.

Now turn around and listen to your hearing essence, are there still so many sounds in it? *Student:* When I get here, all sounds and discriminations are ungraspable.

Marvelous, marvelous . . . You say that when you get here all sounds and all discriminations are totally ungraspable. Since they cannot be grasped, does that not mean there is empty space at such a time? *Student:* Originally not empty, it is clearly not obscure.

What is the substance that is not empty? *Student:* It has no form; there is no way to express it in words.

This is the life of the Buddhas and Zen masters; do not doubt anymore.

CHINUL

As I write this, I hear the street sounds of Manhattan and the rattling of the heating pipes. What do you hear?

357

The
True
Heaven

There are two ways to live your life. One is as though nothing is a miracle. The other is as though everything is a miracle.

ALBERT EINSTEIN

People see God every day; they just don't recognize him.

PEARL BAILEY

The true heaven is everywhere, even in that very place where you stand and walk . . . If man's eyes were opened, he would see God everywhere in this heaven, for heaven stands in the inner-most moving everywhere.

JACOB BOEHME

Life is only this place, this time, and these people right here and now.

VINCENT COLLINS

A recluse, renowned as an enlightened man, came to a heartfelt decision that he was not in fact fully liberated. He thought the Buddha's teaching would help him and he traveled across India until he reached the Buddha's center and asked to see the Buddha. "He is on his begging round," he was told. "Wait here and rest and you will see him soon." "I can't wait," answered the recluse. "Show me the way and I will find him."

He set off for the city center. There he saw the Buddha going with his begging bowl from house to house. The recluse fell to his knees and embraced the Buddha's feet. "You are liberated," he said to the Buddha. "Please teach me a practice that will bring liberation." "Gladly," said the Buddha, "but not here, this is not the time or the place. Go to my meditation center and wait for me." "No, I can't wait. In such a short time I might die or you might die. Now, sir, this is the time. Please teach me now."

The Buddha looked at him and saw that death was near. He realized that the teaching must be given at once . . . "In your seeing," he said, "there should be only the seeing. In your hearing, nothing but the hearing, in your smelling, tasting, and touching, nothing but smelling, tasting, and touching; in your thinking, nothing but the thought."

THE BUDDHA

Go Plainly and Simply

I turn over my little omelet in the frying pan for the love of God. When it is done, if I have nothing to do, I bow down to the ground and adore God from whom has come the grace to make it. Then I straighten up, more contented than a king. When there is nothing more that I can do, it is enough to pick up a straw from the floor for the love of God.

People look for methods for learning to love God. They desire to arrive by I don't know how many different practices. They take great pains to remain in the presence of God by a quantity of means. Is it not much shorter and more direct to do everything for the love of God, to use all the tasks of one's situation, to give testimony to it, and to maintain His presence within us by this communication of the heart with Him? He has no fancy ways for this. One has only to go plainly and simply to Him.

BROTHER LAWRENCE

All Mind

A person goes to sleep in this hall and dreams he has gone on a world-tour, traveling over various continents. After many years of strenuous travel, he returns to this country, enters the ashram, and walks into the hall.

Just at that moment, he wakes up and finds that he has not moved at all but has been sleeping. He has not returned after great efforts to this hall, but was here all the time.

If it is asked, "Why, being free, do we imagine ourselves bound?" I answer, "Why, being in the hall, did you imagine you were on a world tour, crossing desert and sea?"

It is all mind.

RAMANA MAHARSHI

An Endangered Species

[The author of this piece was diagnosed with Lou Gehrig's disease in 1993 and died nine years later.]

I stand at the edge of a life made shorter by illness, and can't help being pulled out of the present moment into mourning my losses, courting my fears. I sigh over my lost prowess as a hula dancer, I fear the day when I will be unable to lift a spoonful of lime Jell-O to my lips. But we all stand at the edge. The present moment is itself an edge, this evanescent sliver of time between past and future. We're called away from it continually by our earthly pleasures and concerns. Even now you may be thinking it's time for another cup of coffee and one of those blueberry muffins. Seems it's always time to be doing something other than what we're doing at the moment. While reading in your chair, you find yourself thinking about last night's argument with your spouse; you're thinking that it's time to rake the leaves, check your e-mail, get some sleep . . .

The present moment, like the spotted owl or the sea turtle, has become an endangered species. Yet more and more I find that dwelling in the present moment, in the face of everything that would call us out of it, is our highest spiritual discipline. More boldly, I would say that our very presentness is our salvation; the present moment, entered into fully, is our gateway to eternal life.

PHILIP SIMMONS

Nirvana and samsara are not two.

MILAREPA

Life is no different from nirvana,
Nirvana no different than life.
Life's horizons are nirvana's:
The two are exactly the same.

NAGARJUNA

The present is not a fleeting moment: it is the only eternity. In
Time "lies" samsara: in the Present "lies" nirvana.

WEI WU WEI

Nothing More, Nothing Less

Who is it that is meditating? If you sit and close your eyes and search forever, you will never find a meditator. For what reason do you meditate?

So while you are there expecting, or even trying to be open for enlightenment, nothing will happen. The anticipation alone is enough to guarantee that. Anticipation is a function of the mind, which is attached to memory of the past and expectations of what will happen in the future. While this is occurring, there can be no possibility of anything else arising. In one way, I can say to you that you can meditate or not meditate; it makes no difference.

When you come to see and understand the nature of "what is," its simplicity, its immediacy, its uniqueness, and its transience, then it is also understood that there is no point in formal meditation. You're sitting at the kitchen table, drinking coffee and the thought comes, "I will go and meditate." Then you see that there is simply no point, because where you are is "what is." What *is* is, and so why go to find it upstairs? When this is embraced, it is possible that it will be recognized that what you are is absolute awareness—nothing more, nothing less.

TONY PARSONS

Just before he passed away at the age of sixty, Bassui sat up in the lotus posture and, to those gathered around him, said:

"Don't be misled!
Look directly!
What is this?"

He repeated this loudly and then calmly died.

BASSUI

This is a great question: What is this? This mind, this self, this life, this moment. What is this?

Live
Here

1. Live now. Be concerned with the present rather than past or future.

2. Live here. Deal with what is present rather than what is absent.

3. Stop imagining. Experience the real.

4. Stop unnecessary thinking. Rather, taste and see.

5. Give in to unpleasantness and pain just as to pleasure. Do not restrict your awareness.

6. Accept no should or ought other than your own. Adore no graven image.

7. Take full responsibility for your actions, feelings and thoughts.

8. Surrender to being as you are.

CLAUDIO NARANJO

[Lawyers Alan Shore and Denny Crane are sitting on their office balcony at the end of a long day, drinking scotch and smoking cigars.]

Alan Shore: You know, one thing I do love about you? While many people embrace the promise of tomorrow, too few celebrate the joy of now, and nobody does that like Denny Crane.

Denny Crane: Well, let me tell you something. When you get polar ice caps melting and breaking off in big chunks, and when you have Osama still hiding in a cave planning his next attack, and when you get other rogue nations with nuclear arsenals, not to mention some whack job home grown who can cancel you at any second. When you got mad cow. . . . *Now* gets high priority. And when you're sitting on the balcony on a clear night sipping scotch with your best friend, *now is everything.*

Alan [toasting his glass of scotch]: Here's to now!

Denny [raising his glass]: Here's to now!

FROM THE ABC TELEVISION SERIES, *BOSTON LEGAL*

Every
Step

Treading along in this dreamlike, illusory realm,
Without looking for the traces I may have left;
A cuckoo's song beckons me to return home,
Hearing this, I tilt my head to see
Who has told me to turn back;
But do not ask me where I am going,
As I travel in this limitless world,
Where every step I take is my home.

DOGEN

This
Morning

This morning I was born again and a light shines in my land
I no longer look for heaven in your deathly distant land
I do not want your pearly gates don't want your streets of gold
This morning I was born again and a light shines in my soul

This morning I was born again, I was born again complete
I stood up above my troubles and I stand on my own two feet
My hand it feels unlimited, my body feels like the sky
I feel at home in the universe where yonder planets fly

This morning I was born again, my past is dead and gone
This great eternal moment is my great eternal dawn
Each drop of blood within me, each breath of life I breathe
Is united with these mountains and the mountains with the sea

I feel the sun upon me, its rays crawl through my skin
I breathe the life of Jesus and old John Henry in
I give myself, my heart, my soul to give some friend a hand
This morning I was born again, I am in the promised land.

WOODY GUTHRIE

Bursting Forth

In standing absolutely still in the midst of our conflicted, conceptual world, we may discover the
explosion of unity, of love, that is the bare actuality of life.

Here is the challenge. Stop. Look. Listen
Nothing is in the way.
Spontaneously, life is bursting forth.

STEVEN HARRISON

Be still and know that I am God.
Be still and know that I am.
Be still and know.
Be still.
Be.

I call this the "Six Line Prayer." The sixth line is my favorite.

Being
Everything

We live in confusion and the illusion of things.
There is a reality.
You are that reality.
When you know that,
you will know that you are nothing,
and, in being nothing,
you are everything.
That is all.

KALU RINPOCHE

Delicious Fragrance

It was as if I had never realized before how lovely the world was. I lay down on my back in the warm, dry moss and listened to the skylark singing as it mounted up from the fields near the sea into the dark clear sky. No other music ever gave me the same pleasure as that passionately joyous singing. It was a kind of leaping, exultant ecstasy, a bright, flame-like sound, rejoicing in itself. And then a curious experience befell me. It was as if everything that had seemed to be external and around me were suddenly within me. The whole world seemed to be within me. It was within me that the trees waved their green branches, it was within me that the skylark was singing, it was within me that the hot sun shone, and that the shade was cool. A cloud rose in the sky, and passed in a light shower that pattered on the leaves, and I felt its freshness dropping into my soul, and I felt in all my being the delicious fragrance of the earth and the grass and the plants and the rich brown soil. I could have sobbed with joy.

FORREST REID

The Whole Teaching

No past,
No future.

Open mind,
Open heart.

Complete attention,
No reservations.

That's all.

SCOTT MORRISON

Sources and Permissions

I want to express my gratitude to all the contributors in this collection for their wisdom. Selections were gathered from books, magazines articles, newspaper interviews, songs, plays, films, poems, personal accounts, audio tapes, transcripts, websites, and private archives. Every attempt has been made to give credit accurately and thoroughly. Any omissions or inaccuracies are inadvertent. For the longer prose and poetry, the necessary permissions are noted. The many shorter pieces are considered fair use under copyright laws. Websites are included so readers can find additional information. I want to thank Fred Courtright and Cathy Gruber of The Permissions Company for their tireless effort in securing the necessary clearances. Sources are alphabetized according to the citations.

A Course in Miracles—*Gifts from a Course in Miracles*, edited by Frances Vaughn and Roger Walsh (Tarcher-Putnam, 1995).

Abbey, Edward, *Desert Solitaire* (Ballantine Books, reissued 1991).

Acocella, Joan, Article: Second Act (New Yorker Magazine, 6 January 2003).

Sources and Permissions

Adams, Robert, *Silence of the Heart* (Copyright © 1987 by The Infinity Institute. Reprinted by permission.); www.robertadams.org.

Adyashanti, *My Secret Is Silence* (Copyright © 2003 by Adyashanti. Reprinted with permission of Open Gate Publishing.); www.zen-satsang.org.

Al-Hallaj, Mansur—poem attributed to Mansur, translator unknown.

Alexander, Christopher, *The Timeless Way of Building* (Oxford University Press, 1979); www.patternlanguage.com.

Almaas, A.H., *The Diamond Heart: Book Three* (Copyright © 1990 by A.H. Almaas) and *The Pearl Beyond Price* (Copyright ©2000 by A. H. Almaas). Both reprinted with permission of Shambhala Publications, Inc.); www.shambhala.com; www.ridhwan.org.

Ardagh, Arjuna Nick, *Wide Awake*, edited by Quidam Green Meyers (The Book Three, 2002); www.livingessence.com.

Baba, Meher, *Discourses* (Copyright © 1987 by Avatar Meher Baba P.P.C. Trust. Reprinted with permission of Avatar Meher Baba Perpetual Public Charitable Trust, Ahmednagar, India. All rights reserved.); www.meherbaba.com.

Babcock, Donald C., "The Little Duck" (*New Yorker Magazine*, 4 October, 1947, vol.23, no.33).

Ball, Alan, *American Beauty* screenplay.

Balsekar, Ramesh S., *A Net of Jewels* (Copyright © 1996 by Ramesh K. Balsekar. Reprinted with permission of Advaita Press.); www.advaita.org; www.ramesh-balsekar.com.

Bamford, Christopher, *In the Presence of Death* (Lapis, 1999. Reprinted with permission of the author.).

Bamidbar, Rabba, *Eyes Made for Wonder*, by Lawrence Kushner (Jewish Lights, 1998).

Bankei, *Bankei Zen*, translated by Peter Haskel (Grove Weidendeld, 1990).

Barbour, Julian, *The End of Time* (Oxford University Press, 1999).

Bassui, *Three Pillars of Zen*, by Philip Kapleau (Copyright ©
1989 by Roshi Philip Kapleau. Reprinted with permission of Doubleday, a division of Random House, Inc.);
Mud and Water by Arthur Braverman (North Point
Press, 1989).

Batchelor, Stephen, *Buddhism Without Beliefs* (Copyright
© 1998 by Stephen Batchelor & The Buddhist Ray,
Inc. Reprinted with permission of Riverhead Books, a
division of Penguin Putnam Inc.).

Bayda, Ezra, Being Zen (Copyright © 2002 by Ezra Bayda. Reprinted with
permission of Shambhala Publications, Inc.); www.shambhala.com.

Beckett, Samuel, *Collected Poems in English and French* (Copyright
© 1961 by Samuel Beckett. Reprinted with permission of
Grove/Atlantic, Inc. and Calder Publishers, Ltd.).

Bennett-Goleman, Tara, *Emotional Alchemy* (Harmony Books, 2001);
www.emotionalalchemy.com.

Berger, John, *The Shape of a Pocket* (Pantheon Books, 2001).

Berger, K.T., *Zen Driving* (Ballantine Books, 1988).

Bhagavad Gita, translated by Stephen Mitchell (Copyright © 2000 by
Stephen Mitchell. Reprinted by permission of Crown Publishing
Group, a division of Random House Inc.); www.stephenmitchellbooks.
com.

Blackburn, Albert, *Now Consciousness* (Idlywild Books, 1983).

Boehme, Jacob, *The Confessions of Jacob Boehme*, translated by
Frederick D. Maurice (Methuen and Company, 1920).

Boorstein, Sylvia, *Pay Attention, for Goodness Sake* (Ballantine
Books, 2002); www.spiritrock.org.

Boston Legal—dialogue excerpt from season 3, episode 28 ("Inde-
cent Proposals") of *Boston Legal*, ABC Television series, written
by Craig Turk, Jill Goldsmith and David Kelley, David E. Kelley
Productions in association with 20th Century Fox Television.

Boucher, Sandy, *Hidden Spring* (Wisdom Publications, 2000);
http://sandyboucher.net.

Sources and Permissions

Brach, Tara, *Radical Acceptance* (Bantam Books, 2003); www.imcw.org.

Brother Lawrence, *Ordinary Graces* (Pickwick Publications, 1989).

Brown, Edward Espe, *Tomato Blessings and Radish Teachings* (Riverhead Books, 1997); www.yogazen.com.

Buddha, "Udana 4:1"; "Samyuta Nikaya, XXXV 23"; "Khuddaka Nikaya"; *The Buddha Speaks* (Copyright © 2000 by Anne Bancroft. Reprinted with permission of Shambhala Publications, Inc. Edited for length); *Connected Discourses of the Buddha* (Wisdom Publications, 2002).

Buechner, Frederick, *Listening to Your Life; Now & Then* (Copyright © 1992 by Frederick Buechner. Reprinted with permission of HarperCollins *Publishers,* Inc. and the Harriet Wasserman Literary Agency, Inc.).

Burroughs, John—www.ecotopia.org/ehof/burroughs/apprec.html.

Capote, Truman, *A Christmas Memor,* (Knopf, 1989).

Carse, James P., *Breakfast at the Victory* (HarperCollins Publishers, 1994).

Chah, Ajahn, *365 Buddha* (Funny Publishing Ltd., 1993).

Chase, Mildred, *Just Being at the Piano* (Creative Arts Books, 1985).

Chinul, *Minding Mind: Secrets of Cultivating the Mind,* translated by Thomas Cleary (Shambhala Publications, 1995).

Chödrön, Pema, *The Places That Scare You* (Copyright © 2001 by Gampo Abbey. Reprinted with permission of Shambhala Publications, Inc.); www.shambhala.com; www.gampoabbey.org.

Chuang Tzu, *The Complete Works of Chuang Tzu,* translated by Burton Watson (Columbia University Press, 1968).

Cohen, Leonard, "Anthem" from *Stranger Music Selected Poems and Songs* (Toronto McClelland & Stewart, 1994); www.leonardcohen.com.

Connor, James A., *Silent Fire* (Crown Publishers, 2002).

Cooper, David A., *The Heart of Stillness* (Bell Tower, 1992).

Cushnir, Raphael, *Unconditional Bliss* (Quest Books, 2000); *Wide Awake*, edited by Quidam Green Meyers (The Book Three, 2002); www.livingthequestions.org.

Daibai, *Zen Poems of China and Japan*, edited by Lucien Stryk, Takashi Ikemoto, and Taigan Takayama (Copyright © 1973 by Lucien Stryk, Takashi Ikemoto, and Taigan Takayama. Reprinted with permission of Doubleday, a division of Random House, Inc.).

Dalai Lama, *The Essence of the Heart Sutra*, translated and edited by Geshe Thupten Jinpa (Wisdom Publications, 2002).

Das, Lama Surya—Reprinted by permission of the author. www.dzogchen.org.

Dass, Ram, *Be Here Now* (Crown Publishers, 1971. Reprinted with permission of the Hanuman Foundation.); *Still Here* (Riverhead Books, 2000); www.ramdasstapes.org.

Data, Omkara—www.coresite.cjb.net.

Davies, Paul, *That Mysterious Flow* (Copyright © 2002 by Scientific American, Inc. All rights reserved.).

De Caussade, Jean-Pierre, *The Sacrament of the Present Moment* (Harper San Francisco, 1982, 1989).

De Mello, Anthony, *Awareness* (Image Books—Doubleday, 1990); *One Minute Wisdom* (Image Books—Doubleday, 1988); www.demello.org.

Deida, David, *Naked Buddhism; Waiting to Love* (Copyright © 2001, 2002 by David Deida. Reprinted with permission of Plexus); info@deida.com, 888-626-9662 www.deida.com.

Deshimaru, Taisen, *The Ring of the Way* (E.P. Dutton, 1983).

Dogen, *Enlightenment Unfolds*, edited by Kazuaki Tanahashi (Copyright © 1999 by San Francisco Zen Center. Reprinted with permission of Shambhala Publications, Inc.); *The Zen Poetry of Dogen*, by Steven Heine (Copyright © 1997 by Steven Heine. Reprinted with permission of the translator; Charles Tuttle publisher.).

Sources and Permissions

Shobogenzo: Zen Essays by Dogen, translated by Thomas Cleary (Copyright © 1986 by Thomas Cleary. reprinted with permission of University of Hawaii Press.).

Dostoyevsky, Fyodor, *The Possessed* (Random House, Modern Library, 1936).

Eckhart, Meister, *Meister Eckhart: A Modern Translation*, translated by Raymond Blakney (Copyright © 1941 by Harper & Brothers. Reprinted with permission of HarperCollins Publishers, Inc.).

Eliot, T.S., *Four Quartets* (Copyright 1940 by T.S. Eliot, renewed © 1968 by Esme Valerie Eliot. Reprinted with permission of Harcourt, Inc. and Faber and Faber, Ltd.); *Ash Wednesday* (Faber and Faber, 1963).

Elliot, Holy Bridges, *Behold God in Many Faces* (St. Mary's Press, 1993).

Emerson, Ralph Waldo, *Self-Reliance*, 1841

Epstein, Mark, *Thoughts without a Thinker* (Basic Books, 1996).

Feldman, Christina, *The Buddhist Path to Simplicity* (Thorsons, 2001); www.gaiahouse.co.uk.

Fenner, Peter—Reprinted with permission of the author; www.wisdom.org.

Foyan, *Instant Zen: Waking Up in the Present*, edited by Thomas Cleary (North Atlantic Books, 1994).

Franck, Frederick, *The Stereopticon* (Copyright © 1997. Reprinted with permission of *Parabola*, the Magazine of Myth and Tradition.).

Freemantle, Francesca, *Luminous Emptiness* (Copyright © 2000 by Francesca Freemantle. Reprinted with permission of Shambhala Publications, Inc.); www.shambhala.com.

Gallagher, Winifred, *Spiritual Genius* (Random House, 2001).

Gampopa, *The Jewel Ornament of Liberation*, translated by Herbert V. Guenther (Shambhala Publications, 1971, Copyright © 1959 by Herbert V. Guenther. Reprinted with permission of Georges Borchardt, Inc.).

Gangaji—www.gangaji.org.

Gita, Ashtavakra, *The Heart of Awareness: Ashtavakra Gita*, translated by Thomas Byrom (Copyright © 1990 by Thomas Byrom. Reprinted with permission of Shambhala Publications, Inc.); www.shambhala.com.

Glassman, Bernie, *Infinite Circle* (Copyright © 2002 by Bernie Glassman. Reprinted with permission of Shambhala Publications, Inc.); www.peacemakercommunity.org; www.shambhala.com.

Goldberg, Natalie, *Thunder and Lightning, Cracking Open the Writer's Craft* (Bantam Books, 2000); www.nataliegoldberg.com.

Goldstein, Joseph, *The Experience of Insight* (Shambhala Publications, Inc., 1987); www.dharma.org.

Goodall, Jane. *Reason for Hope: A Spiritual Journey,* (New York: Warner, 2000), pages 173-74

Gorrell, Donna Lee, *Perfect Madness* (Copyright © 2001 by Donna Lee Gorrell. Reprinted with permission of Inner Ocean Publishing, Inc.).

Gross, Philippe L. and Shapiro, S. I., *The Tao of Photography* (Ten Speed Press, 2001).

Guillevic, *Selected Poems*, translated by Denise Levertov (Copyright © 1968, 1969 by Denise Levertov Goodman and Eugene Guillevic. Reprinted with permission of New Directions Publishing Corporation.).

Gunaratana, Henepola, *Mindfulness in Plain English* (Wisdom Publications, 1993); www.bhavanasociety.org.

Gurdjieff, George I., *Gurdjieff: The Anatomy of a Myth*, by James Moore (Element, 1991).

Guthrie, Woody, "This Morning I Was Born Again" (Copyright © 2000 by Woody Guthrie Publications Inc. Reprinted by permission.); www.woodyguthrie.org.

Gyaltsap, Shechen, *The Spirit of Tibet*, translated by the Padmakara Translation Group (Copyright © 1996 by Padmakara Translation Group. Reprinted with permission of the translator.).

Gyamtso, Tsultrim Khenpo, *The Three Nails, Part II*, translated by Ari Goldfield. Reprinted by Permission (*Bodhi Magazine*, Nov 6–7, 1999); http://ktgrinpoche.org.

Hafiz, *The Subject Tonight Is Love*, translated by Daniel Ladinsky (Copyright © 1996 by Daniel Ladinsky. Pumpkin House Press. Reprinted by permission of the translator.).

Hagen, Steve, *How the World Can Be Like This* (Copyright © 1995 by Steve Hagen. Reprinted with permission of Quest Books/The Theosophical Publishing House, Wheaton, Ill.); www.dharmafield.org.

Hancock, Butch, *Circumstance* (Copyright © 1999 by Two Roads Music (BMI)/Administered by BUG. All rights reserved. Used by permission.).

Hanh, Thich Nhat, *Be Free Where You Are* (Copyright © 2000 by Thich Nhat Hanh. Reprinted with permission of Parallax Press.); *Miracle of Mindfulness* (Beacon Press, 1999); www.plumvillage.org; www.parallax.org.

Harding, Douglas, *Face to No-Face* (Inner Directions Publishing, 2000), www.headless.org.

Hare, David, *The Hours*, screenplay based on the novel by Michael Cunningham (Miramax/Hyperion, 2003).

Harrison, Steven, *Getting to Where You Are* (Tarcher-Putnam, 1999); *The Question to Life's Answers* (Sentient Publications—2002); *Being One* (Sentient Publications—2002); www.doingnothing.com.

Heart Sutra—translation from the Zen Community of New York.

Hendricks, Gay, *A Year of Living Consciously* (HarperSanFrancisco, 1998), www.hendricks.com.

Heraclitus, *Fragments: The Collected Wisdom of Heraclitus*, translated by Brooks Haxton ("Fragment 41"), (Copyright © 2001 by Brooks Haxton. Reprinted with permission of Viking Penguin, a division of Penguin Putnam Inc.).

Hesse, Hermann, *Siddhartha*, translated by Hilda Rosner (Copyright © 1951 by New Directions Publishing Corporation, originally written in 1920).

Hoffman, Albert; *LSD: My Problem Child;* (Tarcher, 1983; reissued in 2005 by MAPS).

Housden, Maria, *Hannah's Gift* (Copyright © 2002 by Maria Housden. Reprinted with permission of Bantam Books, a division of Random House, Inc.).

Howe, Marie, *What the Living Do* (W.W. Norton, 1999).

Huber, Cheri, *There Is Nothing Wrong with You* (Keep It Simple Books, 1993); *That Which You Are Seeking Is Causing You to Seek* (A Center for the Practice of Zen Buddhist Meditation, 1990); www.thezencenter.org.

Hui-Neng, *The Sutra of Hui-Neng*, translated by Thomas Cleary (Copyright © 1998 by Thomas Cleary. Reprinted with permission of Shambhala Publications, Inc.); www.shambhala.com.

Huxley, Aldous, *Island* (Harper and Row, 1962); http://somaweb.org.

Indian Parable, *Wisdom of India: Fairy Tales and Parables* by Heinrich Zimmer.

Ingram, Catherine, *Passionate Presence* (Gotham Books, 2003); www.dharmadialogues.org.

Ionesco, Eugene—phrases from the play *Exit the King,* 1962.

Jakushitsu, Genko, *A Quiet Room: The Zen Poetry of Zen Master Jakushitsu*, translated by Arthur Braverman (Copyright © 2000 by Arthur Braverman. Reprinted with permission of Charles E. Tuttle Co., Inc. of Boston, Massachusetts and Tokyo, Japan).

Jesus, *The Gospel of Thomas*, translated by Stephen Mitchell. Reprinted with permission of the translator; *The Gospel of Thomas*, the Nag Hammadi Library, stanzas 113 and 3, edited by James M. Robinson (HarperCollins, 1978, 1988).

Johnson, Spencer, *The Precious Moment* (Copyright © 1981 by Spencer Johnson. Reprinted with permission of Doubleday, a division of Random House, Inc.).

Sources and Permissions

Joko Beck, Charlotte, *Everyday Zen* (Harper San Francisco, 1989).

Joshu, *The Recorded Sayings of Zen Master Joshu*, translated by James Green (Shambhala Publications, 1998).

Jourdain, Stephen, *Radical Awakening* (Inner Directions Publishing, 2001).

Kabat-Zinn, Jon, *Wherever You Go, There You Are* (Hyperion, 1994); www.mindfulnesstapes.com.

Kabir, *The Kabir Book*, translated by Robert Bly (Copyright © 1977 by Robert Bly. Reprinted with permission of the translator.).

Kalu Rinpoche, *The Message of the Tibetans* by Arnaud Desjardins (Stuart and Watkins, 1969); www.kdk.org.

Kane, Ariel and Shya, *Working on Yourself Doesn't Work* (ASK Productions, 1999); www.ask-inc.com.

Katie, Byron, *Loving What Is*, written with Stephen Mitchell (Harmony Books, 2002); www.thework.com.

Kaye, Les, *Zen at Work* (Crown Trade Paperbacks, 1996); www.howardwade.com/kannon_do/kdo.html.

Kazantzakis, Nikos, *Zorba the Greek*, translated by Carl Wildman (Scribner/Simon & Schuster, 1952, renewed 1981).

Keating, Thomas, *An Interview with Thomas Keating* (*Parabola*, the Magazine of Myth and Tradition, February 1990); www.centering prayer.org.

Keizan, *The Record of Transmitting the Light*, translated by Francis Dojun Cook (Center Publications, 1981); *Transmission of Light*, translated by Thomas Cleary (North Point Press, 1990).

Kerouac, Jack, *The Scripture of the Golden Eternity* (Copyright © 1960 by Jack Kerouac. Reprinted with permission of City Lights Books.).

Keyes, Roger, "Hokusai Says," reprinted by permission of the author.

Khema, Ayya, *Be an Island* (Wisdom Publications, 1999).

Khen, Nyoshul, *Natural Great Perfection*, translated by Lama Surya Das (Copyright © 1995 by Surya Das. Reprinted with permission of Snow Lion Publications.).

Khyentse, Dilgo, *The Hundred Verses of Advice of Padampa Sangye*, translated by Padmakara Translation Group (Copyright © 2002. Reprinted with permission of Shambhala Publications, 2004); www.shechen.org.

Kim, Jae Wong, *Polishing the Diamond*, translated by Yoon Sang Han (Wisdom Publications, 1999).

Kitchens, James A., *Talking to Ducks* (Fireside Book/Simon and Shuster, 1994).

Klein, Jean, *The Ease of Being* (The Acorn Press, 1981); www.jean klein.org.

Ko Un, *Beyond Self*, translated by Young-Moo Kim and Brother Anthony (Copyright © 1997 by Young-Moo Kim and Brother Anthony. Reprinted with permission of Parallax Press); www.parallax.org.

Koestler, Arthur, *The Invisible Writing* (Beacon Press, 1954).

Kornfield, Jack, *The Art of Forgiveness, Lovingkindedness, and Peace* (Copyright © 2002 by Jack Kornfield. Reprinted with permission of Bantam Books, a division of Random House, Inc); *After the Ecstasy, the Laundry* (Bantam Books, 2000); www.spiritrock.org.

Krishnamurti, J., *On God* (Copyright © 1992 by Krishnamurti Foundation Trust, Ltd. and Krishnamurti Foundation of America. Reprinted with permission of HarperCollins Publishers, Inc); *In the Light of Silence and Surely, Freedom from the Self* (Reprinted with permission of the Krishnamurti Foundation Trust); www.kfa.org, www.kfoundation.org.

Kushner, Lawrence, *God Was in This Place and I Did Not Know* (Copyright © 1998 by Lawrence Kushner. Reprinted with

Sources and Permissions

permission of Jewish Lights Publishing, P.O. Box 237, Woodstock, VT 05091); www.jewishlights.com.

Lama Shabkar, *The Flight of the Garuda*, translated by Keith Dowman (Wisdom Publications, 1994).

Lerner, Marc, "Holding Silence's Hand" (Reprinted with permission of the author); marclerner@ lifeskillsinc.com.

Levine, Stephen, *A Year to Live; Healing into Life and Death* (Copyright © 1997 by Stephen Levine. Reprinted with permission of Bell Tower, a division of Random House, Inc.).

Levitt, Peter, *100 Butterflies* (Broken Moon Press, Copyright © 1992 by Peter Levitt. Reprinted with permission of the author.).

Lilly, John—www.johnclilly.com.

Lin-Chi (Rinzai), *Zen Teachings of Master Lin-Chi*, translated by Burton Watson (Columbia University Press, 1999).

Locker, Thomas, *Walking with Henry* (Copyright © 2002 by Thomas Locker. Reprinted with permission of Fulcrum Publishing).

Loy, David, *Non-Duality* (Humanity Books, 1988 and 1998).

Lozoff, Bo, *It's a Meaningful Life* (Viking, 2000); www.humankindness.org.

Lucille, Francis—from the unpublished manuscript *Eternity Now*; www.francislucille.com.

Lusseyran, Jacques, *And There Was Light*, translated by Elizabeth R. Cameron (Parabola Books, Copyright © 1963 by Elizabeth R. Cameron. Reprinted with permission of Little, Brown and Company.).

Ly Ngoc, Kieu, *Women in Praise of the Sacred*, translated by Thich Nhat Hanh and Jane Hirshfield (Copyright © 1994 by Thich Nhat Hanh and Jane Hirshfield. Reprinted with permission of HarperCollins Publishers, Inc. and Michael Katz.).

Maezumi, Taizan, *Appreciate Your Life: The Essence of Zen Practice* (Copyright © 2001 by White Plum Asanga, Inc. Reprinted with permission of Shambhala Publications, Inc.); www.shambhala.com; www.zcla.org.

Magid, Barry, *Ordinary Mind* (Wisdom Publications, 2002); www.ordinarymind.com.

Maharaj, Nisargadatta, *I Am That*, edited by Sudhakar S. Dikshit and translated by Maurice Frydman (The Acorn Press, 1973); *Nectar of Immortality*, edited by Robert Powell (Blue Dove Press, 2001); www.nisargadatta.net.

Maharshi, Ramana, *Talks with Sri Ramana Maharshi* (T.N. Venkataraman, 1989); *The Essential Teachings of Ramana Maharshi* (Inner Directions Publishing, 2001); www.ramana-maharshi.org.

Main, John, www.wccm.org.

Manson, Herbert, *The Death of al-Hallaj* (University of Notre Dame Press, 1979)

Marshall, Bart, "What Is Realized?" from Tat Forum website.

Maslow, Abraham, *Religions, Values, and Peak Experiences* (Viking, 1970); www.maslow.com.

Matthiessen, Peter, *The Snow Leopard* (Viking, 1978).

Maung, U Kyi, *Instinct for Freedom* by Alan Clements (New World Library, 2002).

McEwan, Ian, "Joy" from *Hockney's Alphabet*, drawings by David Hockney with written contributions edited by Stephen Spender (Random House in association with American Friends of AIDS Crisis Trust, 1991).

McLeod, Ken, *Wake Up to Your Life* (HarperCollins, 2001); www.unfetteredmind.org.

Merton, Thomas, *In Silence: The Collected Poems of Thomas Merton* (Copyright © 1977 by Abbey of Gethsemani. Reprinted with permission of New Directions Publishing Corporation.); www.merton.org.

Merton, Thomas, Conjectures of a Guilty Bystander (Copyright 1965 by Thomas Merton, Doubleday).

Metzger, Deena, *Looking for the Faces of God* (Copyright © 1989 by

Deena Metzger. Reprinted with permission of Parallax Press.); www.parallax.org.

Miller, Arthur, *After the Fall* (Penguin Edition, 1964, 1992).

Miller, Henry, *Standing Still Like the Hummingbird* (New Dimension Book, 1962); *The Wisdom of the Heart* (New Directions, 1941); *Plexus* (Grove Press, 1987); www.henrymiller.org.

Mitchell, Stephen, "The Answer" from *The Wishing Bone* (Candlewick Press, 2003).

Morissette, Alanis, lyrics from "Thank U" (Ballard/Morissette ©1999. Reprinted by kind permission of Universal/MCA Music Publishing. A.D.O. Universal Studios Inc.).

Morrison, Scott, *The Gentle Art of Not-Knowing* (Renaissance Memes, LLC, 2000, Reprinted with permission.); www.openmindopenheart.org.

Moss, Richard—Reprinted with permission of Richard Moss; www.richardmoss.com

Nagarjuna, *Mahamudra* by Takpo Tashi Namgyal (translation Copyright © 1987 by Lobsang Lhalungpa. Reprinted with permission of the translator. Shambhala Publications.); *Verses from the Center*, translated by Stephen Batchelor (Copyright © 2000 by Stephen Batchelor. Reprinted with permission of Riverhead Books, an imprint of Penguin Putnam Inc.).

Nakagawa, Soen, *One Bird, One Stone*, by Sean Murphy (Renaissance Books/St. Martin's Press, 2002); www.murphyzen.com.

Naranjo, Claudio, excerpted from "Present-Centeredness in Gestalt Therapy," in Fagan, Joe N., and Irma Lee Sheperd, eds., *Gestalt Therapy Now* (Palo Alto, CA: Science and Behavior Books, Inc., 1970).

Norris, Gunilla, *Journeying in Place* (Bell Tower/Harmony, 1994).

Nouwen, Henri J. M., *Here and Now* (Crossroad, 1994, 1997); http://nouwen.net.

Nyima, Chokyi, *Indisputable Truth* (Copyright © 1996 by
Chokyi Nyima Rinpoche, translated by Erik Pema
Kunsang. Reprinted by permission of Rangjung Yeshe
Publications.); www.choklingtersar.org; www.she
drub.org; www.rangjung.com.

Oliver, Mary, *New and Selected Poems* (Copyright ©
1992 by Mary Oliver. Reprinted with permission of
Beacon Press.).

O'Neill, Eugene, *Long Day's Journey into Night* (Copyright © 1956 by
Eugene O'Neill. Reprinted with permission of Yale University
Press.).

Orme-Johnson, David W.—Submission #00048 from The Archive of
Scientists' Transcendent Experiences (TASTE), managed by and
reprinted by permission of Dr. Charles T. Tart; www.issc-
taste.org.

Osho, *What Is, Is, What Ain't, Ain't* (1980); *Ah This!* (2001),
Reprinted with permission of Osho International Foundation;
www.osho.com.

Packer, Toni, *The Light of Discovery* (Copyright © 1999 by Toni
Packer. Reprinted with permission of Charles E. Tuttle Co., Inc.
of Boston, Massachusetts and Tokyo, Japan); *The Wonder of
Presence* (Shambhala Publication, 2002); *A Quiet Space* (Spring-
water Center Newsletter, Fall 2001. Reprinted with permission of
the author.); www.springwatercenter.org.

Padmasambhava, *Self-Liberation through Seeing with Naked Awareness*, by John Myrdhin Reynolds (Snow Lion Publications, 2000).

Pai-Chang, *The Teachings of Zen*, translated by Thomas Cleary
(Barnes & Noble, and Shambhala Publications, 1998).

Parsons, Tony, *As It Is* (Inner Directions Foundations, 2000);
www.theopensecret.com.

Patrul Rinpoche, *Buddha Mind*, translated by Tulku Thondup Rinpoche (Snow Lion Publications, 1989); *Simply Being* (Vajra
Press, 1994, 1998).

Sources and Permissions

Pessoa, Fernando, *Poems of Fernando Pessoa*, translated and edited by Edwin Honig and Susan M. Brown (Copyright © 1986 by Edwin Honig and Susan M. Brown. Reprinted with permission of City Lights Books.).

Phillips, Jan, *God Is at Eye Level* (Quest Books, 2000); www.janphillips.com.

Pirsig, Robert, *Zen and the Art of Motorcycle Maintenance* (William Morrow, 1974).

Po, Huang, *The Zen Teachings of Huang Po*, translated by John Blofeld (Grove Press, 1958).

Poonja, H. W. L., *The Truth Is*, compiled by Prashanti De Jager (Samuel Weiser, 1995–2000); *Nothing Ever Happened, Volume 3*, by David Godman (Avadhuta Foundation, 1998); www.poonja.com.

Powell, Robert, *Dialogues on Reality* (Blue Dove Press, 1996).

Rabbin, Robert, *The Sacred Hub* (The Crossing Press, 1996); www.robrabbin.com

Reid, Forrest, *Following Darkness,* (London: Arnold, 1902).

RERU—Archived experiences (#1263, #1802, #1916, #3670, and #4440) from the Religious Experience Research Centre, Alister Hardy Trust, Department of Theology and Religious Studies, University of Wales, Lampeter. Reprinted by permission of the Alister Hardy Trust; some accounts appeared in *Seeing the Invisible* by Meg Maxwell and Verena Tschudin (Penguin Group, 1991), and *Common Experience* by J. M. Cohen and J. F. Phipps (Random Century Group Ltd., 1992); www.alisterhardytrust.org.uk.

Ricard, Matthieu, and Trinh Xuan Thuan, *The Quantum and the Lotus* (Crown Publishers, 2001); www.shechen.org; www.padmakara.com.

Richmond, Lewis, *Work as Spiritual Practice* (Broadway Books, 1999); www.lewisrichmond.com.

Rilke, Rainer Maria, *Letters to a Young Poet*, translated by Stephen

Mitchell (Copyright © 1986 by Stephen Mitchell.
Reprinted with permission of Random House, Inc.);
The Selected Poetry of Rainer Maria Rilke, edited and
translated by Stephen Mitchell (Random House, 1982);
www.stephenmitchellbooks.com.

Rohr, Richard, *Radical Grace* (St. Anthony's Messenger
Press, 1995).

Rosenberg, Larry, *Living in the Light of Death* (Copyright
© 1986 by Larry Rosenberg. Included with permission of Shambhala Publications, Inc.); www.shambhala.com;
http://members.bellatlantic.net/~vze4b9v8.

Rosenberg, Marshall B. (PhD)—Founder of Center for Nonviolent
Communication. Reprinted with permission of author;
www.cnvc.org.

Rothenberg, David, *Blue Cliff Record: Zen Echoes*, (Copyright ©
2001 by David Rothenberg. Reprinted with permission of Codhill
Press.)

Rumi, *The Essential Rumi*, translated by Coleman Barks with John
Moyne (HarperCollins/Castle Books, Copyright © 1995 by Coleman Barks and John Moyne. Reprinted with permission of Coleman Barks); *Rumi: In the Arms of the Beloved*, translated by
Jonathan Star (Copyright © 1997 by Jonathan Star. Reprinted
with permission of Penguin Putnam Inc.).

Sacks, Oliver, *A Leg to Stand On* (Touchstone/Simon & Schuster,
1984); www.oliversacks.com.

Sahn, Seung, *Compass of Zen*, compiled by Hyongak and Seung Sahn
(Shambhala Publications, 1997); *Dropping Ashes on the Buddha*,
edited by Stephen Mitchell (Grove Press, 1994);
www.kwanumzen.com.

Salt, Henry S., *Life of Henry David Thoreau* (University of Illinois
Press, 1993).

Salinger, J. D., "Teddy" from *Nine Stories* (Little, Brown and Company,
Copyright renewed © 1981 by J. D. Salinger, originally published
1953. "Teddy" first appeared in *The New Yorker*).

Salzberg, Sharon, *Faith* (Riverhead, 2002); *The Cabbage Sutra* (Tricycle Newsletter. Reprinted by permission of author); *A Heart as Wide as the World* (Shambhala Publications, 1997); www.dharma.org.

Sanders, Scott Russell, *Staying Put* (Beacon Press, 1993).

Sarriugarte, Tracy D., and Peggy Rose Ward, *Making Friends with Time* (PBJ Publishing, 1999).

Segal, William, *Opening* (Copyright © 1998. Reprinted with permission of Continuum International Publishing Group Inc.).

Seixas, Abby, *Find the Deep River Within* (Jossey-Bass, 2007).

Seng Ts'an, *Zen Chinese Heritage*, translated by Andy Ferguson (Wisdom Publications, 2000).

Sexton, Anne, *The Awful Rowing toward God* (Copyright © 1975 by Loring Conant, Jr., Executor of Estate of Anne Sexton. Reprinted with permission of Houghton Mifflin Company and Sterling Lord Literistic, Inc. All rights reserved).

Shainberg, Lawrence, *Ambivalent Zen* (Pantheon Books, 1995).

Shankar, Vijai S. Dr.—www.ksashram.org.

Shapiro, Isaac, *The Teachers of One*, edited by Paula Marvelly (Watkins Publishing, 2002); www.isaacshapiro.de.

Shapiro, Rami M., *Meditation from the Heart of Judaism* (Copyright © 1997 by Avram Davis. Reprinted with permission of Jewish Lights Publishing, P.O. Box 237, Woodstock, VT 05091); www.jewishlights.com.

Shen-ts'an, *Transmission of the Lamp: Early Masters*, compiled by Tao Yan and translated by Sohaku Ogata (Weatherhill, Inc., April 1997).

Shi Tou, *Zen Chinese Heritage*, translated by Andy Ferguson (Wisdom Publications, 2000); *The Roaring Stream: A New Zen Reader*, edited by Nelson Foster and Jack Shoemaker (Ecco Press, 1996).

Shiyu, *Meditating with Koans*, translated by J. C. Cleary (Asian Humanities Press, 1992); www.jainpub.com.

Shoshanna, Brenda, *Zen Miracles* (John Wiley and Sons, 2002); www.brendashoshanna.com.

Shulman, Alix Kates, *Drinking the Rain* (Copyright © 1995 by Alix Kate Shulman. Reprinted with permission of Farrar, Straus & Giroux, LLC.); www.alixkshulman.com.

Shulman, Jason, *The Master of Hiddenness* (A Society of Souls, 1999), www.kabbalah.org.

Simmons, Philip, *Learning to Fall* (Copyright © 2002 by Philip Simmons. Reprinted with permission of Bantam Books, a division of Random House, Inc.); www.philipsimmons.org.

Smith, Huston, *The World's Religions* (HarperCollins, 1991).

Stafford, William, *The Way It Is: New and Selected Poems* (Copyright © 1991, 1993, 1998 by Estate of William Stafford. Reprinted with permission of Graywolf Press.).

Steger, Manfred B., and Perle Besserman, *Grassroots Zen* (Copyright © 2001 by Manfred B. Steger and Perle Besserman. Reprinted with permission of Charles E. Tuttle Co., Inc. of Boston, Massachusetts and Tokyo, Japan.).

Steindl-Rast, David, and Sharon Lebell, *Music of Silence* (Seastone, 1998; 2002).

Stuart, Maurine, *Turning Wheel*, Spring 1990.

Suzuki, D. T., *Zen Buddhism* (Doubleday/Anchor, 1956).

Suzuki, Shunryu, *Crooked Cucumber*, by David Chadwick (Broadway Books, 1999); *Not Always So* (HarperCollins, 2002); www.sfzc.com.

Ta Hui, *Swampland Flowers: The Letters and Lectures of Zen Master Ta Hui*, translated by Christopher Cleary (Copyright © 1977 by Christopher Cleary. Reprinted with permission of Grove/Atlantic, Inc.).

Tarrant, John, *The Light inside the Dark* (HarperCollins, 1998); www.pacificzen.org.

Taylor, Jill Bolte, *My Stroke of Insight: A Brain Scientist's Personal Journey* (Copyright © 2006 by Jill Bolte Taylor, Viking Adult, 2008 edition), www.drjilltaylor.com and see her video talk at www.ted.com.

Thomas, Abigail, *A Three Dog Life: A Memoir* (Harcourt, 2006).

Thoreau, Henry David, *Thoreau on Man and Nature* (Peter Pauper Press, 1960); *Walking* (HarperSanFrancisco, 1994).

Thorp, Gary, *Sweeping Changes* (Walker and Company, 2000).

Titmuss, Christopher, *The Awakened Life* (Shambhala Publications, 2000); www.insightmeditation.org.

Tolle, Eckhart, *The Power of Now* (Copyright © 1999 by Eckhart Tolle. Reprinted with permission of New World Library); www.newworldlibrary.com; www.eckharttolle.com.

Tolle, Eckhart, *Stillness Speaks* (New World Library, 2003).

Trungpa, Chögyam, *Meditation in Action* (1991); *Cutting through Spiritual Materialism* (1973); *The Myth of Freedom* (2002), Shambhala Publications, Inc.; www.shambhala.org.

Tsoknyi, Drubwang, *Carefree Dignity* (Copyright © 1998 by Tsoknyi Rinpoche, translated by Erik Pema Kunsang and Marcia Binder Schmidt. Reprinted with permission of Rangjung Yeshe Publications.); www.pundarika.org; www.rangjung.com.

Tsoknyi, Drubwang, *Fearless Simplicity* (Copyright © 2003 by Tsoknyi Rinpoche and Rangjung Yeshe Publications), compiled and translated by Erik Pema Kunsang and Marcia Binder Schmidt.

Tsu-hsin, *The Teachings of Zen*, edited by Thomas Cleary (Barnes and Noble, 1998).

Tsun ba je gom, *Buddhism without Beliefs*, by Stephen Batchelor (Riverhead, 1997); www.martinebatchelor.org/stephenbio.html.

Urgyen, Tulku, *Rainbow Painting; As It Is, Volume I*, both translated by Erik Pema Kunsang (Copyright © 1996, 1999 by Tulku Urgyen

Rinpoche. Reprinted with permission of Rangjung
Yeshe Publications); www.rangjung.com.

von Baeyer, Hans Christian, *Maxwell's Demon* (Random
House, 1999).

Wagoner, David, *Traveling Light* (Copyright © 1999 by
David Wagoner. Reprinted with permission of University of Illinois Press and the author.).

Walker, Alice, *The Color Purple* (Pocket Edition, 1990).

Watts, Alan, "This Is It" from *The Way of Liberation* (Vintage Books,
1973); www.alanwatts.com.

Watzlawick, Paul, *How Real Is Real?* (Vintage Books, 1976).

Wei, Wei Wu, *Walking through the Mirage;* www.weiwuwei.8k.com.

Welch, Lew, *Ring of Bone: Collected Poems 1950–1971* (Copyright ©
1973. Reprinted with permission of Grey Fox Press.).

Whitman, Walt, *Leaves of Grass* (The Modern Library, 2001).

Whyte, David, *Where Many Rivers Meet* (Copyright © 2000 by David
Whyte. Reprinted with permission of Many Rivers Press.);
www.davidwhyte.com.

Wiederkehr, Macrina, *Seasons of the Heart: Prayers and Reflections*
(HarperCollins, 1991).

Wilber, Ken, *The Eye of Spirit; One Taste: The Journals of Ken
Wilber; Grace and Grit* (Copyright © 1998, 1999, 1993 by Ken
Wilber. Reprinted with permission of Shambhala Publications,
Inc.); www.shambhala.com.

Wren-Lewis, John, "The Dazzling Dark" from *What Is Enlightenment*
magazine and material from an upcoming book. Reprinted with
permission of the author.

Wright, James, "Today I Was Happy, So I Made this Poem" from
Above the River: The Complete Poems (Copyright © 1963 by
James Wright. Reprinted with the permission of Wesleyan Univer-
sity Press.).

Wu-men, *The Enlightened Heart*, edited and translated by Stephen

Sources and Permissions

Mitchell (Copyright © 1993 by Stephen Mitchell. Reprinted with permission of Harper Collins.).

Yerachmiel, Ben Yisrael Reb, *Open Secrets: The Letters of Reb Yerachmiel Ben Yisrael*, translated and edited by Rami M. Shapiro (Human Kindness Foundation, 1996. Reprinted with permission of author.).

Young, Shinzen. Reprinted with permission of author. www.shinzen.org.

Yuanwu, *Zen Wisdom*, translated by Thomas Freke (Godsfeld Press, 1997); *Zen Letters: Zen Master Yuanwu*, translated by J. C. Cleary and Thomas Cleary (Shambhala Publications, 1994).

Yun-feng, *The Teachings of Zen*, translated by Thomas Cleary (Shambhala Publications, 1998).

Zaleski, Irma, *The Door of Joy* (Copyright © 1998. Reprinted with permission of *Parabola*, the Magazine of Myth and Tradition.).

Acknowledgments

I gratefully dedicate this book to Tulku Urgyen, who kindly introduced me to the nature of mind, and to Byron Katie, whose gift of inquiry showed me a new way to live an awakened life in every moment.

I want to express my special thanks to all those who contributed to the birth and evolution of this book: my agent, Michael Katz; Edmund Mercado for his tireless work managing all the pieces; my generous editors—Joel Heller, Victor Davich, Reed Moran, and Carol Williams; and my friends who shared their feedback and support—Raphael Cushnir, Susan Piver Browne, Stephen Mitchell, Kate Lila Wheeler, Dr. Joe Siegler, Craig Smith, Alan Gensho Florence, Loch Kelly, Terry Patten, Steven Sashen, Rande Brown, Bill McKeever, Amy Gross, Mark Matousek, Catherine Ingram, Lama Surya Das, James Shaheen, Bill Higgins, and Sharon Salzberg.

Thanks to my kind publishing collaborators at both Element and Hampton Roads: Greg Brandenburgh, Belinda Budge, Jacqueline Burns, Carole Tonkinson, Steven Fischer, Matthew Cory, and Simon Gerratt.

Acknowledgments   I acknowledge and thank my mentors over the years: Tsoknyi Rinpoche, Mingyur Rinpoche, Khenpo Tsultrim Gyamtso, Nyoshul Khen Rinpoche, Patricia Sun, Helen Palmer, Jiyu Roshi, and the many sages who inspired me but whom I never met in person. My gratitude to the wise friends, teachers, masters, writers, authors, poets, and artists, whose wonderful insights grace these pages.

I am grateful to the publishers and authors who allowed their writings to be included: Shambhala Publications, Rangjung Yeshe Publications (Erik and Marcia Schmidt), Wisdom Publications, Snow Lion Publications, Parallax Press, Religious Experience Research Centre, Coleman Barks, Open Gate Publishing, Riverhead Books, Crown Publishing, Doubleday, Dr. Marshall B. Rosenberg, Gary Rosenthal, Stephen Mitchell, Plexus, Charles E. Tuttle Co., Parabola Magazine, Peter Fenner, New Directions, the Padmakara Translation Group, Quest Books, Bantam Books, Robert Bly, City Lights Books, the Krishnamurti Foundation Trust, Jewish Lights Publishing, Bell Tower, Peter Levitt, Little, Brown and Company, HarperCollins, New Directions Publishing, Renaissance Memes, Richard Moss, Lobsang Lhalungpa, Beacon Press, Dr. Charles Tart, Osho International Foundation, Toni Packer, Codhill Press, Penguin Putnam, Continuum International Publishing Group, Houghton Mifflin, Farrar, Straus & Giroux, Graywolf Press, Grove/Atlantic, New World Library, University of Illinois Press, University of Hawaii Press, Many Rivers Press, Grey Fox Press, John Wren-Lewis, and Rabbi Rami M. Shapiro.

About the Author

Josh Baran has been actively involved in Buddhism, meditation, and mindfulness for nearly five decades, beginning when he was sixteen years old. He spent seven years in a Zen community becoming a monk, priest, and teacher. Since the early 1980s, he has been a strategic communications and public affairs specialist, first in Los Angeles and then in New York City. Over the years, he has worked with nonprofit organizations, foundations, and companies including the Pediatric AIDS Foundation, Amnesty International, NRDC, GLAAD, Special Olympics, Microsoft, Oracle, Paramount Pictures, Universal Pictures, HBO, Fox Searchlight, Miramax, the Sundance Film Festival, Time Warner, Warner Records, Random House, and many others. He is well known for handling the strategic outreach for controversial films and documentaries. For many years, he managed media relations for the visits of the Dalai Lama to the eastern United States. He also directed communications for the visits of the Tibetan leader the 17th Karmapa, B. K. S. Iyengar, S. N. Goenka, and Mingyur Rinpoche.

Hampton Roads Publishing Company

. . . for the evolving human spirit

Hampton Roads Publishing Company publishes books
on a variety of subjects, including spirituality,
health, and other related topics.

For a copy of our latest trade catalog, call (978) 465-0504
or visit our distributor's website at *www.redwheelweiser.com*.
You can also sign up for our newsletter and special offers
by going to *www.redwheelweiser.com/newsletter/*.